THE HUMAN FACTOR IN BUSINESS

THE HUMAN FACTOR IN BUSINESS

FURTHER EXPERIMENTS IN INDUSTRIAL DEMOCRACY

BY

B. SEEBOHM ROWNTREE

AUTHOR OF
"POVERTY", "THE HUMAN NEEDS OF LABOUR", ETC.

WITH ILLUSTRATIONS

LONGMANS, GREEN AND CO.
LONDON   ♦   NEW YORK   ♦   TORONTO

LONGMANS, GREEN AND CO. LTD.
39 PATERNOSTER ROW, LONDON, E.C.4
17 CHITTARANJAN AVENUE, CALCUTTA
NICOL ROAD, BOMBAY
36A MOUNT ROAD, MADRAS

LONGMANS, GREEN AND CO.
114 FIFTH AVENUE, NEW YORK
221 EAST 20TH STREET, CHICAGO
88 TREMONT STREET, BOSTON

LONGMANS, GREEN AND CO.
215 VICTORIA STREET, TORONTO

First Published 1921
Second Edition 1925
Third Edition 1938

PRINTED IN GREAT BRITAIN BY J. AND J. GRAY, EDINBURGH

PREFACE TO THE THIRD EDITION

IN 1921 I published a book, with the above title, in which I gave an account of the principles underlying the labour policy at Rowntree's Cocoa Works in York, England, and of the steps taken to implement them.

In 1925 I published a second edition of the book, bringing the information up to date.

The information there given is now, in its turn, quite out of date, and as we are constantly being asked what we are doing in relation to this or that labour problem, I decided to prepare another edition. But I have found it necessary almost entirely to re-write the book—for two reasons, first, because in the last thirteen years many of the practices fully described in my previous book are now so commonly employed that it seemed unnecessary to dwell on them in detail, and second, because matters relating to the human factor in business which were relatively unimportant in 1925 are very important to-day, and I have felt it necessary to discuss them at much greater length.

I do not think it is generally realised how profound is the change which has taken place since the war in the workers' attitude to industrial conditions. During the war, millions of them, both men and women, were shaken out of the ruts in which they had been living and working, and they were not content to return to them when the war ended. They no longer took the old conditions for granted ; they demanded something better. Hitherto they had concerned themselves principally with material conditions, such as wages and hours of work, but after the war, while vigorously pressing their demands in connection with these matters, they began seriously to question the status normally accorded to workers under our industrial system. This new point of view was well put by the late Mr. Harry Gosling at a Trade Union Congress in 1916.

" We are tired," he said, " of war in the industrial field. The British workman cannot quietly submit to an autocratic government of the conditions of his own life. He will not take ' Prussianism ' lying down, even in the dock, the factory, or the mine. Would it not be possible for the employers of this country . . . to put their businesses on a new footing, by admitting the workmen to some participation not in profits but in control ? We workmen do not ask that we should be admitted to any share in what is essentially the employer's own business—that is, in those matters which do not concern us directly, in the industry or employment in which we may be engaged. We do not seek to sit on the board of directors, or to interfere with the buying of materials, or with the selling of the product. But in the daily management of the employment in which we spend our working lives, in the atmosphere and under the conditions in which we have to work, the conditions of remuneration, and even in the manners and practices of the foreman with whom we have to be in contact ; in all these matters we feel that we, as workmen, have a right to a voice—even to an equal voice— with the management itself. Believe me, we shall never get any lasting industrial peace except on the lines of industrial democracy."

The views expressed by Mr. Gosling are widely held by the workers, and the demand to be treated

as co-operators in industry[1] rather than merely as
servants, is growing day by day. No system of labour
management will succeed which does not take this
demand of the workers fully into account. The
directors at the Cocoa Works have all along felt that
this demand of the workers was a fair one, and have
sought to meet it as far as possible. In the first chapter
of this book I describe, in considerable detail, the steps
which have been taken in this direction. I think we
have succeeded in large measure in changing the
workers' status to that of co-operators, and have
done so without lowering efficiency, and I hope that
this record of our experiments may be of interest
to others who are working in the same field.

Following the chapter on status is one dealing with
remuneration, in which I describe the close co-operation which exists between the management and the
workers in determining what should constitute a fair
day's work. In that chapter I also deal with the subject of profit sharing and the guarantee given against
cutting piece rates. The next chapter deals with
economic security. I am not sure whether to-day the
workers generally would not regard the economic
insecurity which is so marked a feature of modern
industry as " Public Enemy Number One." The
experiments that we have tried with a view to lessening
this insecurity are described. Some of them have met
with a measure of success, but others—notably those
concerned with the insecurity arising from the risk
of unemployment—have been only very partially
successful. Then follows a chapter on hours of work,
where the subject of a shorter working week is discussed. We have been working a five-day week since

[1] Here and throughout this volume I use the word "industry"
to cover not only manufacturing but also agriculture, mining, transport, and the distribution of goods. I recognise, however, that
although the principles involved apply throughout, their detailed
application will vary.

1919. A further chapter describes the organisation of our labour department, and another deals with what are usually described as " welfare conditions." These conditions are important in themselves, but are secondary in importance to such fundamental matters as status, remuneration, and economic security. Finally, there is a chapter in which the questions dealt with in the previous chapters are briefly summarised, and the significance of the experiments described is assessed.

I have received much help from many of my colleagues at the Cocoa Works in the preparation of this little book, and to them I tender my grateful thanks. Especially I would thank Mr F. G. Fryer, the Vice-Chairman of the Company, who has succeeded me as Labour Director at York, also the Labour Manager, Dr C. H. Northcott, and Miss K. Sherlock, Mr H. W. Locke, and Mr B. P. Rowntree, who are members of his staff.

I would also on behalf of the directors as a whole take this opportunity to thank all those executives and leading representatives of the workers, who by their sympathy and understanding have made it possible to carry out the policy here described.

B. S. R.

North Dean,
High Wycombe, Bucks,
September 1938.

INTRODUCTION

WHATEVER may be the conscious motives which induce any given individual to engage in industry, its basic purpose must always be the service of the community, for without industry and commerce the community would starve in a few days. It was because men could only exist if they worked, that they engaged in industry. A little effort on their part enabled them to subsist ; greater effort enabled them to live in greater comfort. So we may say that the basic purpose of industry is to create goods and provide services of such kinds, and in such measure, as may be beneficial to the community. But under any satisfactory industrial system two conditions must be observed :

(1) In the process of wealth production, industry must pay the greatest possible regard to the general welfare of the community and pursue no policy detrimental to it.

(2) The wealth produced must be distributed in such manner as will best serve the highest ends of the community.

These conditions may be difficult of attainment, but I do not think they can be regarded as unreasonable. None of us would seriously attempt to defend a proposition that industry, as a whole, should be conducted with a view to rendering a small section of the community rich and powerful, regardless of the welfare of the rest of the people. I might go further and say that none would defend a proposition that it would be right for industry to be conducted primarily in the interests of a small group without reasonable regard for the rest of the community.

But when we speak of " industry as a whole," what we really have in mind is a vast number of individual enterprises. Remove those and nothing is left, and, therefore, the principles on which " industry as a whole " should be conducted are applicable to each industrial unit, and this places a heavy responsibility on all employers. I can well imagine that there are many industrialists who say they are not interested in abstract questions ; that it is as much as they can do to attend to their own business and make it as success-ful as they can. But for industrialists to ignore con-sideration of the broad principles on which industry should be conducted is to adopt a short-sighted policy, because whether they are interested in these basic principles or not, the fact remains that millions of people are interested in them, and are becoming increasingly determined that industry shall be con-ducted for the benefit of the community as a whole. Until comparatively recently, workers accepted the capitalistic system as an established fact, and confined their efforts to making the best bargains that they could with employers. But, to-day, vast numbers of them no longer take the present industrial system for granted.

If I read the situation rightly, they are not so much interested in abstract social theories, as increasingly filled with a sense that, in the past, society has given them, on the whole, a " raw deal." They desire two things : better material conditions, and an improved status in industry. I do not think there are many who would quarrel with these desires. The desire for improved material conditions is universal, though it takes different forms in different circumstances. It is certainly active to-day in Britain, and probably in every industrialised country throughout the world, and I think it is likely to remain so.

The demand for improved status follows a different course. There may be no active demand for it among certain primitive peoples, where all men are more or less equal under a single chief whose authority is unquestioned, though strictly limited. But society, as it develops, tends to become stratified into classes. The classless society of the savage develops by gradual steps into one more complex. We find, for instance, societies consisting of three groups : freemen working for themselves, masters, and slaves. In time, slavery gives place to serfdom, and serfdom to freedom. But for most this freedom is qualified. It is not the freedom of the savage—who calls no man his master save his chieftain, but rather the freedom to choose one's occupation and one's master. Even this freedom is much more restricted to-day than it was before the industrial revolution. In all highly industrialised countries industry tends, with ever-increasing momentum, to become concentrated in large enterprises. Retail trade is falling more and more into the hands of multiple stores and co-operative societies, and manufacture into those of large limited liability companies, or amalgamations of companies, sometimes of gigantic size. The same tendency is showing itself in agriculture, where the smallholder finds it increasingly hard to succeed, for farmers of mixed farms are, to an ever-growing extent, entering the fruit, vegetable, and poultry industries, which were hitherto exclusively the preserves of smallholders.

Thus, though the workers have won legal freedom, the vast majority of them find themselves in the position of servants. Through legislation, or the activities of trade unions, a measure of protection which is often considerable is enjoyed against exploitation ; but even allowing for this, it is true that their status in large measure is that of mere servants rather than co-operators. To-day, they are beginning to rebel against this state of things. Every week in Britain hundreds of meetings are held at which the workers are told that all the means of production, distribution, and exchange should be nationalised, and controlled by the workers. Their position under the present industrial system of industry is portrayed as being wage slavery ; and not only labour propagandists, sometimes referred to as " labour agitators," but also a growing number of earnest men and women who do not belong to the working-class and are solely actuated by altruistic motives, are urging the workers to unite and gain political power through the ballot box, so that they may replace the capitalistic system of industry by socialism.

It is far from my intention in this book to express any political views. What I want to do is to impress upon my readers, and especially on my fellow-employers, that *no system of industry can be defended, nor will it endure, unless it not only is capable of serving but actually serves the interests of the community as a whole at least as well as any practical alternative.*

Therefore, I submit that all those who control industry should give serious thought to the answers which can be given to the following questions :—

Is it possible under the existing industrial system—

(1) to give good service to the consumer ?

(2) to provide conditions for the workers of all grades comparing not unfavourably with those they might reasonably expect to enjoy under any other industrial system ?

(3) and, having done these things, to make business pay ?[1]

[1] I do not deal here with the question whether the hardships caused by competition between business units can, under the com-

This book is chiefly concerned with question number two, but I may briefly refer here to the others.

As to the first, in the absence of trade monopolies (which can be dealt with, if necessary, by legislation), competition among producers and suppliers of services ensures good service to the consumers. In spite of the waste incidental to the present system, I believe its advantages far outweigh its disadvantages so far as the consumer is concerned.

The question whether compliance with conditions (1) and (2) would impose upon industry so heavy a burden that, under existing economic conditions, it could not function profitably, is one which cannot be briefly answered, but under any system every branch of industry must either " pay " or be scrapped, or be subsidised by the community. Several industries in this country and elsewhere are to-day being helped either by direct Government subsidy or by other means. Therefore, we have already conceded the principle that if an industry is worth retaining, it can, if necessary, be subsidised from public funds. It is, however, important to remember that in the long run the community can only pay subsidies out of profits earned in industry or commerce, and, therefore, the proportion of the country's industry which can be subsidised is strictly limited. I see no reason to suppose that industries will need more help under the present system than under any other.

Many employers to-day fight shy of providing better

petitive system, be so regulated that they do not outweigh its advantages to the communal well-being, since as a matter of fact, the whole of this question stands on a different footing from the other three. If any of those could not be answered in the affirmative, the probability is that public opinion would very soon demand that a system which was incapable of serving the highest ends of the community must be changed ; but injury done to individual enterprises or shareholders under the present system would not be likely to arouse public opinion to a degree which would lead to a demand for the system to be changed for their benefit.

conditions for their employees because of the cost. But the expense as shown in the trading account is misleading. The money spent is shown to the last penny, but nothing appears on the credit side of the account to show the gain to the business arising from having a happier, healthier, and more co-operative staff. If only it were possible to show how much hard cash the country loses day in and day out, not merely through strikes and lock-outs, or days lost through illness, but through lack of full co-operation from the workers, and because many of them " enjoy only poor health," I am certain that we should be amazed, and our attitude to many of the questions discussed in this book might very likely be changed.

It is often assumed that " welfare " methods can only be introduced into businesses which through good luck or good management, or both, are particularly profitable, but that is quite a mistake. A struggling business may not be in a position to *give* additional advantages to its employees, but wise leadership may well enable those to be *earned*. I have seen some of the best welfare conditions in very simple little factories. There were no extravagant canteens or medical services or recreation grounds, but there was a spirit of comradeship between employer and employed. The workers knew that their interests were wrapped up in those of the employer, and that they could count on their prosperity growing with his. They knew, too, that in all fundamental matters their needs and their views would be regarded with understanding and sympathy, and I am sure that the workers in those factories would not have changed places with others in factories having costly welfare equipment, but in which the spirit of friendship and camaraderie was absent.

It is, therefore, wrong to assume that improvements in labour conditions necessarily involve expense.

Some of the most valued will cost nothing in £. s. d. Where expenditure is involved it is equally wrong to assume that such expenditure cannot in due course yield a corresponding return. Nevertheless it is obviously true that businesses cannot suddenly adjust themselves to substantial increases in wages or important improvements in conditions. Changes should be made gradually, and time given for managerial efficiency and close co-operation between the management and the workers so to develop as to carry the extra expenditure.

But one must recognise the difficulty of the individual employer in an industry where labour conditions are generally bad. Such an employer can go only a certain way in advance of his competitors. However, he may find on investigation that he may be able to carry most of his competitors along with him; indeed, that they are as anxious to go as he, and at any rate in certain important directions the majority may be able to deal with the minority by, for example, the establishment of a Trade Board. This, however, is too large a question to deal with here.

As stated, this book deals with question number two. It sets forth the efforts made in a large factory to afford to the workers good working conditions and a worthy status. Although in writing about these I have had in mind the question of whether, under a competitive system, it is possible to afford to the workers conditions as good as they could reasonably expect to enjoy under any alternative system, I want to make it quite clear that in making the experiments here described the directors never had in mind a comparison between the conditions they were seeking to establish and those which might be possible under any other system ; nor did they make the experiments because they were actuated by any fear that unless considerable changes in industrial practice were made the present industrial system would be upset. In the case of our factory, as in the case of hundreds of others where experiments on more or less similar lines have been made, the purpose of the directors has been merely to establish the best conditions that they could.

The book is not written in any spirit of self-advertisement : indeed, the directors are very conscious how far the practices they have so far found themselves able to adopt fall short of their ideals, and they would be inclined to say, with Browning, " Oh, oh ! It makes me mad to see what men shall do, and we in our graves ! " They have, however, learned much from experiments made by others, and believe that the rate of social progress is advanced, if those working in similar fields will make known the results of any experiments they have made.

ILLUSTRATIONS

CONTENTS

THE HUMAN FACTOR IN BUSINESS

CHAPTER I

THE WORKERS' STATUS

In the introduction I said that the workers desire two things from industry—better material conditions and an improved status. I deal with the latter first, because the experiments we have made in this field affect the whole of our labour policy.

Broadly, it may be said that in framing that policy our objective has been to raise the status of the workers of all ranks from that of servants to that of co-operators ; in other words, to introduce into the management of the business, in all matters directly affecting the workers, as great a measure of democracy as possible without lowering efficiency. But as one of the questions considered in this book is whether, in the matter of status, as in other matters, it is possible to afford to the workers conditions as good as they might reasonably expect under any other industrial system, let us, before describing the steps we have taken to improve the workers' status, ask what kind of status workers might reasonably expect to enjoy under a socialist or communist system of industry, for it is one of these which they have in mind when they think of alternatives to capitalism. Not until we know this can we say whether it would be possible to give them as good a status under capitalism.

In seeking an answer to our question, we cannot divorce a claim for a good status from the necessity for efficiency in industry, for if industry is inefficiently conducted the standard of life of the workers will necessarily be low. They will not be satisfied with an industrial system unless it affords them both a good status and a satisfactory standard of living. Bearing this in mind, I suggest that most thoughtful workers would accept the following propositions :—

(1) Under any system of industry, every enterprise must be conducted efficiently. This involves that, so far as possible, every employed person, whether an executive or a manual worker, shall work at the task and under the conditions which will enable him to make his greatest contribution to the success of the enterprise.

(2) No business can be efficiently managed by mass meetings of the workers. The workers must be divided into those whose duty it is to give orders and those whose duty it is to obey them. Orders must be given by individuals, not by committees.

(3) The " order givers " should be selected by those best qualified to do so, and they should be chosen because among all the available candidates for the posts they are those who can make the greatest contribution to the success of the enterprise.

(4) Managerial policy should be devised by those best qualified to do so. Thus in the case of large enterprises the financial policy should be devised by financial experts, the marketing and sales policies by marketing and selling experts, the labour policy by experts on labour questions, and so on.

It will be noted that in framing these propositions I

assume that the organisation of industry must be such as will enable it to function efficiently. I think that in visualising their status under socialism and communism, workers do not make sufficient allowance for the restrictions on the liberty of individuals which must necessarily be imposed in the interests of efficiency. But if, on the one hand, workers may have to modify their ideas of the status they would enjoy under socialism, employers, on the other hand, must bear in mind that the four conditions laid down *could* be observed under a socialist system of industry, and that if they *were* observed, the status of the workers would undoubtedly be better than is common to-day. It is therefore incumbent on them to ask whether they can be observed under capitalism.

No employer will quarrel with the proposition that no business can be efficiently managed by mass meetings of the workers, but it will be seen that carrying out the proposition that every employed person shall work at the task which will enable him to make his greatest contribution to the success of the enterprise means that when selecting men or women for jobs, their personal qualifications should be the only consideration taken into account. There should be no nepotism, no class or racial distinction. This, after all, is not unreasonable, since a high standard of industrial efficiency is essential to a high standard of living for the workers, and this is true whether we are speaking of industry as a whole or of a particular enterprise. Thus to fill executive posts with men of second-rate ability, not because they are the best men available, but because they are the relatives or protégées of directors or other privileged persons, is an injustice to the shareholders, to the workers in the enterprise, and to the community as a whole.

The third proposition, dealing with the question of who is to choose the business executives, also necessitates important modifications in present practice, for undoubtedly it involves giving the rank and file workers a say in the selection of some of the " order givers."

The conditions laid down in the fourth proposition providing for managerial policy being devised by men having the necessary expert knowledge would also involve modifications in present usual practice ; for in the field of labour policy this expert knowledge is most likely to be valuable if employees, through suitably selected representatives, are given a say in the labour policy of each enterprise.

So far as status is concerned, I do not believe that there is any widespread demand for anything more than is consistent with the full observance of these four propositions. Of course, there is a small minority who are out to " smash capitalism," and who will be satisfied with nothing short of this. But such men only fish successfully in troubled waters ; they will not gain adherents save among discontented workers.

The great mass of the workers are perfectly willing to leave both appointments and policy concerned with finance, markets, and so forth to experts in these matters ; and the same is true, though not quite to the same extent, of the various problems connected with production. Here individual workers not infrequently can make useful contributions to knowledge and efficiency, and they feel that they are treated not as co-operators but just as servants, if they are not afforded opportunity to do so.

But when it is a question of labour matters and working conditions, not only are they vitally interested, but they have expert knowledge. If the shoe pinches, they know just *where* it pinches. They therefore demand that they shall take part in the selection of those executives who directly control their working conditions, and also in framing business policy, where this is directly concerned with labour matters.

I think it is possible under the capitalist system to comply with the conditions outlined in my four propositions, and in this and following chapters I describe how far we have been able to go in this direction.

It will help us to appreciate the significance of the different steps that have been taken to meet the demand of the workers, if we remember that that demand is, in effect, one for a greater measure of democracy in the control of industry, and then to bear in mind what are the essential features of democracy.

May we not state these as follows ? Under democracy—

(1) The people make their own laws.

(2) They have a say (though often a very indirect one) in the appointment of those who administer the laws.

(3) They are protected by impartial Courts of Justice against unfairness in their administration.

(4) They are at liberty to express their views freely either by word of mouth or in writing.

In this chapter I shall describe the steps taken to democratise our scheme of management at the Cocoa Works under four headings :—

The Making of Lwas.

The Selection of Persons to administer them.

Protection against Unjust Administration of the Laws.

Freedom of Speech.

THE MAKING OF LAWS

In considering the growth of democratic methods of fixing wages and working conditions, we may draw a broad distinction between steps taken to fix these for a whole industry or for a group of firms within the industry and those taken to fix them for a particular enterprise. In the chapter on Wages, I describe how these are fixed in the chocolate industry—minimum wages and conditions applicable to the whole industry by a Trade Board, and a higher scale of wages and better conditions by an Interim Industrial Reconstruction Committee,[1] membership of which is voluntary.

The fixing of minimum wages enforced by law and the creation of bodies such as the Interim Industrial Reconstruction Committee represent a great advance upon the time when wages and working conditions were virtually fixed by autocratic employers, and the workers had no alternative but to accept them or starve. But important though agreements governing a large number of firms are, the development of democracy makes itself even more intimately felt when one comes to consider the close watch which a strong and energetically organised trade union keeps over the interests of its members in individual enterprises. Not only are the unions constantly working to secure higher wages, shorter hours, and improved working conditions, but they take steps to ensure that agreements which have been come to are kept by the individual employer, and that individual workers are protected against measures which they regard as unjust.

It might be argued that if workers are members of an effective trade union, they already enjoy a status in industry which should satisfy any reasonable person ; but anyone who has an intimate knowledge of industry, whether from the standpoint of an employer or a worker, knows that such an argument is unsound. However powerful a union may be, it cannot possibly take up the case of every worker who feels that he has

[1] See p. 45.

a grievance. Nor can it do very much to create a spirit
of true co-operation between employers and employed.
I do not want to minimise what a trade union can do in
this matter, and what some of the best-managed ones
are doing, but their secretaries would be the first to
admit that their methods must necessarily be those of
" mass production," whereas what is really needed, if
a true spirit of co-operation is to be developed in a
factory, is to give detailed attention to a great number
of matters each of which may be small in itself, but
which in the aggregate are of great importance.
But while the amount of detailed attention which the
unions can give within a particular factory is necessarily limited, they can do and are doing much to
encourage employers and employed in individual
factories to work out such methods together. Indeed,
I should like to testify here to the help given in this
direction by almost every one of the unions with
which I have had to deal during the last thirty years
or so. Especially, I should like to acknowledge the
help given in this connection by the National Union
of General and Municipal Workers, to which almost all
the workers, other than tradesmen, in the factory
belong. Our relationships with the unions, ever since
they began to organise our workers, have always been
cordial ; and for many years past, notices have been
posted up in the works encouraging workers to join
their respective unions. At the present time, these
are worded as follows and signed by the chairman of
the York Board of Directors :—

TRADE UNIONS

We have been informed that a number of employees would like to know what is the attitude of
the Directors to Trade Unions.

While recognising that it is entirely a matter for

the employee's own judgment as to whether he shall or shall not join a Trade Union, the opinion of the Directors is " *that it is desirable in the interests of the Company and its employees that the latter shall be suitably organised, and that membership of a Trade Union is, in the general case, desirable.*"

We never inquire whether an employee is or is not a member of a union, but I know that almost all the factory workers, and the majority of the clerical staff, are trade unionists.

While unions, quite naturally and rightly, seek to secure the best terms they can for workers in matters of wages, hours, and general working conditions, I have almost invariably, and always in the case of the National Union of General and Municipal Workers, found them willing to look at both sides of a question. We have succeeded in discussing any differences that might arise between us in a friendly and reasonable spirit, and I hope that both parties have always felt that fair and reasonable decisions had been reached.

Of course, if reason is expected from a trade union, reason must be offered first. An employer who does not recognise the right of the workers to negotiate with him about any matter concerned with their wages or working conditions on even terms through their union officials, or who seeks to dictate terms to the workers, either individually or through their unions, cannot expect them to show a reasonable spirit in negotiation.

To summarise the part which trade unions play in building up a spirit of co-operation between capital and labour, it may be said that they help to lay the foundations on which the structure of co-operation may be built. But after they have done all that is possible, an enormous amount remains to be done in each individual factory, and the extent to which this is successful will depend, first of all, upon whether the methods adopted are wisely chosen, and, secondly, on whether those seeking to operate them are actuated by a truly co-operative spirit. I pass, therefore, from the work of the trade unions to that of steps taken in our own factory to develop democratic methods of management.

As already stated, the object of the directors is and has for long been to introduce as much democracy into the management of the business as can be done without lowering efficiency. They want to reach a point where every one employed, no matter in what position, not only regards himself as a co-operator in a joint effort to render the business successful, but regards every one else in the same light. It is an ideal which is difficult of attainment, but both the management and the rank and file workers have for years been striving together to advance on the road to its attainment, and they are encouraged by the results so far obtained.

The first essential to the creation of a spirit of co-operation is full and frank consultation on all matters affecting the workers' daily life within the factory. This is not only desirable in itself, but forms a preliminary step to any more specific sharing of responsibility.

THE WORKS COUNCILS

Of course, to consult the workers on industrial conditions is not a new policy in factories. We had done so informally and frequently for many years before we sought to establish a more definite system of consultation through works councils. This was introduced some time before the appointment, in 1917, of the Government committee generally known as the

Whitley Committee,[1] and long before its reports were published.

When first we suggested the inauguration of councils at the Cocoa Works, our proposal was looked at very doubtfully by the unions, who thought that the effect might be to undermine their authority. The matter was fully discussed with them, and eventually they were persuaded that the unions would not be weakened, if it was understood that if a decision were come to with which they did not agree, it should not be acted upon until the matter had been discussed with them. Further, the secretary of the local branch of the trade union to which the majority of our workers belong, receives in advance a copy of the agenda of all meetings of the central council, and may attend them if he wishes, but without a vote. Experience has shown that the fears originally entertained by the unions have not been justified, and in fact the union secretary has only attended on two occasions.

I will not weary the reader by describing in detail the experiments which we have made. Briefly, however, it may be said that in the beginning we set up a threefold system. First, there were sectional councils which were concerned solely with matters affecting clearly defined sections of the workers, all of whom were engaged on similar or closely allied processes, and were working in the same department. Representatives from sectional councils sat on departmental councils, which considered matters affecting a department as a whole, and departmental councils sent representatives to a central works council, which dealt with matters affecting the whole factory. Experience showed, however, that this system was too

---

[1] This was a committee appointed by the Government to study the relations between employers and employed. Its chairman was the late Right Hon. J. H. Whitley. Among other things it recommended the setting up of "Joint Industrial Councils" in the better organised industries. These came to be known as Whitley Councils.

unwieldy. Often the work to be done by the sub-sidiary councils was so trivial that the workers took but little interest in it and felt that the whole scheme was somewhat artificial ; moreover, the total number of persons taken from work to attend the councils was out of proportion to the value of the ends gained. After a short experience we therefore abolished sectional councils altogether, and reduced the numbers on the departmental councils. Simultaneously, we made a system of shop steward [1] representation an integral part of our arrangements, a step to the consequences of which I shall have to refer in a moment.

There are now thirteen departmental councils, each consisting of approximately equal numbers of the administrative staff and of rank and file workers. The workers' side consists in the first place of the shop stewards, who are *ex officio* members. The balance of the workers' representatives are elected by ballot of all the workers in the different departments who have been in the company's employment for six months or more and are over eighteen years of age. Thus neither membership of the council nor voting in their election is (apart from shop stewards) confined to trade unionists, but, as a non-unionist would stand but little chance of election, it may be said that the councils are substantially trade union bodies so far as the representation of the workers is concerned. The num-bers on the councils vary, the idea being that there shall be a representative of each defined section of workers, so that if any question arises as to particular conditions, someone will be present who can speak with knowledge of the kind of work

---

[1] Shop stewards are those members of trades unions who are elected by their fellow trade unionists to act on their behalf in any matter which may arise between the workers and the management in the department in which they work.

affected.[1] The administrative representatives on the departmental councils are not elected, but are appointed by the management. In choosing them, the aim is to select those whose presence is most necessary or will best facilitate the prompt and satisfactory handling of matters arising. So far, however, as can be done consistently with this aim and the size of the council, the different grades of administrative officers are given representation. The council meetings are held during working time ; day workers are paid their ordinary wages during the time they spend in meetings, and piece-workers receive their average piece-rate earnings.

At first the councils met every month, but gradually much of the work they originally did came to be done informally by conferences between the management and the shop stewards, so that now the departmental councils only meet occasionally when there are special matters to bring before them.[2] We have more than once considered whether in view of this the departmental councils still fulfilled a useful function or whether they had become unnecessary. The shop stewards are always available, and complaints and proposals can be made through them expeditiously, without waiting for a council meeting. The executive committee of the central council have on several occasions considered this matter, and have discussed it in detail with the departmental councils, and their recommendation, which has been adopted, was that the departmental councils should continue. They recognised that a large number of subjects which at one time came before them are now dealt with through the shop stewards, and that meetings need be less

[1] Including members of the administrative staff, six councils have twelve members or less, seven have between fifteen and twenty members, and one has twenty-two.

[2] During the three council years ending February 1938, four of the thirteen councils met fourteen times or more, five met between nine and twelve times, and four less than nine times.

frequent than formerly, but they felt that there is
still a place for councils—

(1) where matters of principle or of major importance affecting not only individuals but the whole
department may be discussed;

(2) where the management may broadcast a
knowledge of departmental plans, developments,
hopes, and difficulties, and receive constructive
criticism; and

(3) where representation can be given to non-
unionists and overlookers, and a place of contact
thus maintained for all grades and sections, so that
tolerance and sympathy with one another's problems
and points of view can be engendered.

The central council consists of twenty-six administrative representatives, partly elected by different
grades of management and partly appointed by the
board, and thirty workers' representatives, appointed
by the workers' representatives on the departmental
councils. It forms a focus for the work of the departmental councils, and deals with broad questions
affecting the works as a whole. It meets about eight
times a year; the chairman is elected by the meeting
and has no casting vote. It is a standing rule that the
chairman shall be selected from the workers' and the
administrative sides alternately. There is no limit
set to the subjects which may be raised either at the
departmental or central council meetings, except that
matters of purely departmental interest and merely
personal grievances may not be raised at the central
councils. Basic working conditions laid down in
the agreement drawn up by the Interim Industrial
Reconstruction Committee are also ruled out; if either
party desires the alteration of these conditions, they

must apply to the national committee. The central council could, however, request the national committee to consider such alteration. All decisions of the council, whether central or departmental, are subject to the veto of the board of directors on the one hand, and that of the trade unions on the other. Since, however, the councils consist of approximately equal numbers of administrative officers and rank and file workers, the board of directors and the unions would hesitate, without good reason, to veto a decision which had been approved by a large majority. At the meetings of the central council (where the most important matters are discussed) the director members often take upon themselves the responsibility of finally agreeing to matters settled in the council. If they were in doubt they would bring the matter up at the next board meeting, and inform the central council if exception had been taken to its decision. Similar action would be adopted by the trade unions if occasion should arise. I can recall only two occasions on which a decision of the council has been vetoed either by the unions or by the directors.

Probably the size of the central council will be criticised. Obviously, if it were much smaller, matters could be discussed in greater detail. On the other hand, thirty workers is not a large number to represent a body of 10,000. The detailed work is done by sub-committees, and, on the whole, I think that the sense of co-operation would be lessened if the representation were decreased. Some difficulty has been experienced in familiarising the workers generally with the activities of the councils ; a summary of the minutes is put on the departmental notice boards, but this hardly solves the problem. The matter is, however, not one of great moment ; in the case of all important matters, news of what has been said and done at the meetings soon spreads through the works.

MATTERS DEALT WITH BY COUNCILS

It may help the reader if, before leaving the question of councils, I give a few illustrations of the kind of questions with which they deal.

I take, first, as an example, one of the departmental councils. Each year as soon as possible after its election the newly formed council draws up a permanent agenda of items to be discussed as a matter of routine at each regular meeting. Other unforeseen items are, of course, included as they arise. The permanent agenda for 1938–9 is as follows :—

(1) Report from a departmental representative on the central works council.

(2) Imperfect work (mis-shapes and " throw-outs ").

(3) Methods of safeguarding the purity of the ingredients used in the company's goods.

(4) Means of safeguarding the goods from foreign substances and ensuring hygienic conditions.

(5) Departmental collections.

(6) Statement by the manager, who reports on the company's trade, particularly as it affects the department. New and existing lines are shown and suggestions for improving them or their get-up are invited. This occasionally leads to constructive suggestions. Particulars are given of any lines withdrawn.

(7) *Suggestions.*—Particulars are given of suggestions received from workers in the department, and any direction in which improvements or ideas are particularly wanted is mentioned by the management. This often leads to useful discussions, one suggestion made in the course of discussion leading to others.

(8) *Accidents.*—Particulars of any accidents which

have occurred since the previous meeting are given with a view to keeping the members " safety first " conscious and to stimulating constructive suggestions for reducing the risk of accidents.

(9) *Theft.*—Report of any thefts which have occurred since the previous meeting, with a view to reducing theft by fostering a healthy public opinion on the subject and by devising methods for eliminating undue temptation to steal.

It will be seen that more than half the items on the permanent agenda bear directly on production problems. Attendance at one of the departmental councils is sufficient to show how keen an interest is taken in the questions raised, and how real is the contribution made by the workers.

The central council deals principally with matters affecting the whole factory. Since its formation it has dealt with matters of great importance to the workers, such as the following :—

(1) Revised all existing works rules. Any addition to these, or revision of existing rules, must be agreed by the council before they become operative. (See p. 20.)

(2) Decided, subject to the approval of the trade unions, to accept the directors' offer to reduce the length of the working week from 47 to 44 hours on terms suggested by them. (See p. 90.)

(3) The directors left it to the council to decide how the working hours should be apportioned over the week. The council arranged for a plebiscite of the workers, who elected to work the 44 hours in five days, and thus have Saturdays free.

(4) Decide annually when the works holiday shall be taken.

(5) Proposed to the management that the workers

should have a say in the appointment of over-lookers. (For action taken, see p. 22.)

(6) The central council was asked to approve the appointment of a works psychologist : his proposed functions were explained, and a committee was appointed to consider the matter. After lengthy consideration, the committee recommended that the council should agree to the appointment upon certain conditions, one of which was that the person to be appointed, and his sphere of work, should be approved by a joint committee. This report was ultimately adopted and a joint committee appointed to carry out its recommendations.

(7) *Theft.*—A committee was appointed to confer with the director concerned, with a view to discovering the best method of dealing with cases of theft, and of creating a sound public opinion on the matter in the works. (For action taken, see p. 26.)

(8) At the request of women's representatives, the company's policy with regard to the employment of temporary women workers was discussed (there was discontent amongst the women because the employment of temporary labour reduced overtime).

(9) Discussion of board's proposal to inaugurate a profit-sharing scheme, and collaboration in its formulation.

(10) The same with regard to an unemployment benefit scheme, and other similar cases.

Although we are here considering the part which the councils play in determining the working conditions, or, in other words, the part which they play as " law makers," this will be the most convenient place in which to refer to other matters with which they also deal. They frequently discuss questions concerned with production. For instance :—

B

(1) At one meeting, at the request of the workers' representatives, it was decided that discussions should take place between the workers and the production director with a view to seeing whether improvements could be made in quality, designs of boxes and labels, cleanliness, display, packing, visitors' tours of the factory, research, and transport.

(2) The council chairman (a worker) raised the question of waste of energy, time, and material which the workers alleged was taking place. Criticisms and suggestions put forward were considered by the competent authorities ; and at the next meeting of the council, their detailed replies were placed before it by the production director, and a useful discussion followed, when certain misapprehensions with regard to policy concerning quality and waste, etc., were cleared up.

(3) Arising out of a trade statement by the company chairman, at the workers' suggestion a committee of workers was appointed to co-operate with the management in seeking to reduce the costs of production, improve the quality and increase the sales of a certain line which showed a sales decline. This co-operation was welcomed by the management. A sub-committee of workers was set up—

(*a*) To find ways of economising in packing, so that more value might be given in the chocolates.

(*b*) To suggest new designs for the chocolates.

(4) In a food factory, constant care has to be exercised to prevent foreign substances getting into the chocolate in the course of manufacture. The council thoroughly investigated this problem, and at its instigation suggestions were sent in

by the various departmental councils. These suggestions were thoroughly examined by the production director and the departmental managers, and in many cases adopted.

(5) Periodically, the theft committee[1] reports on cases of pilfering which have occurred in the factory, and much thought has been given by the council to means of checking it.

And lastly, the council deals with what may be described generically as welfare matters, such as education, canteen, recreation, and so on.

It will thus be seen that the council is not a " window dressing " affair, but deals with matters which vitally affect working conditions. Notwithstanding the fact that the board of directors and the trade unions reserve the right to veto any decisions come to, they have, as already stated, scarcely ever exercised it.

Apart from questions settled with the trade unions, many of which are dealt with either in the Trade Board or the Interim Industrial Reconstruction Committee, all questions of importance which directly affect the workers are brought to the councils for discussion before being decided on.

Making Laws

So far, in considering the extent to which working conditions at the Cocoa Works are determined by democratic methods, I have referred to the parts played by the Trade Board, the Interim Industrial Reconstruction Committee, and the trade unions, all of which operate from outside the works. I have also described the organisation of works councils within the factory and indicated the kind of subjects with which they deal. Now I pass on to describe the

[1] See p. 26.

character of some of the important measures which
have been established after full discussion in the
central council. If I were speaking of a country
instead of a factory, I should say that I was going
to describe some of the more important social measures
which had been passed by Parliament.

To my mind, the most important single step which
has been taken to democratise government at the
Cocoa Works is the manner in which works rules
are made. In 1923 the directors, realising that
almost all the works rules, many of which had been
operating for years, had been made without consultation with the workers, decided to take the workers'
views upon them. They therefore proposed to the
central council that the whole list of rules should
be revised by a committee consisting of four workers
elected by the workers' side of the council and four
administrative officers appointed by the directors.
This committee went through the rules in detail,
suggesting modifications in some cases, but not making
any drastic changes. They submitted their report to
the central council, where it was considered at some
length, and subsequently a set of rules was unani-
mously agreed to by the workers and the administrative officers. No objection having been raised to
this list of rules either by the board of directors or the
trade unions, they were signed by the chairman and
vice-chairman of the central council. From that
moment it could truly be said that all the laws of
the factory had been drawn up by democratic means.
I remember that when the committee was first
appointed to review the rules, someone in the council
asked whether some step should not be taken to
overcome the difficulty which would arise if the
committee arrived at a deadlock, since it consisted
of equal numbers of workers and administrative
officers. The answer given was that such a difficulty

might be dealt with when it arose. It is now fifteen years since it was decided that all rules should be made by the management and the workers, acting jointly, and on no single occasion has there been any difficulty in arriving at agreement upon rules and alterations of rules. Sometimes there is considerable discussion, and different views are expressed, but always agreement has been reached which both parties have felt to be fair.

Appointing Administrators of Laws

I stated earlier that under democracy people not only make their own laws, but they appoint (directly or indirectly) the officers who administer them. I have just described how far we have gone at the Cocoa Works in introducing the first condition of democracy, and now I pass on to describe how far we have gone in meeting the second one.

Before attempting to answer this question, we must ask : " In the appointment of which administrative officers do the workers desire to have a say?" Setting aside those individuals who, largely on theoretical grounds, desire to control industry from top to bottom, I think it may be safely stated that it is the overlookers, *i.e.* the foremen and forewomen, in whose appointment the workers want to have some say—indeed an equal say—with the management, because it is with them that they come into daily, almost hourly contact, and it is they, more than anyone else, who can render a worker's life in the factory agreeable or miserable. I do not believe there is any general desire on the part of the workers to be consulted with regard to the appointment of higher officers, and certainly not of any of the officers dealing with technical matters.

In the Cocoa Works we have confined the appointment of administrative officers by democratic means to the appointment of overlookers. The question was first raised at one of the departmental works councils when a proposal was made by a worker that when a vacancy occurred in the overlooking staff of a department, the council of that department should have the right to make the appointment, subject to the final veto of the directors. After lengthy discussion at different meetings, it was finally agreed that when an overlooker is to be appointed, the management would consult with a small committee of the workers in the departmental council concerned. This committee was to be a small one, usually consisting of two people, who were pledged to secrecy with regard to what took place at the committee meetings. The procedure agreed to was for the manager of the department to inform this committee whom he nominated to fill the vacant post, and to take their opinion on his proposal. If they agreed right away, then the matter was settled. Sometimes they said they were doubtful and would like time to consider the name ; on a few occasions they have at once raised objections to the name brought forward. In those cases, they were asked to suggest another name or names, and any names suggested were reviewed by the manager and the workers on the committee together. When this system was introduced, the directors were afraid that the workers might press the claims of men who were popular, but who did not possess the administrative qualifications necessary to make a good foreman, and, therefore, they reserved the right to have the last word if the manager and the workers could not agree. However, they have always succeeded in coming to an agreement, so the directors have never had to exercise the right which they reserved. To-day, instead of two members of the departmental council conferring with the manager, the shop steward represents the workers. It has thus proved possible, to this extent, for the " appointment of officers to administer the laws " to be made on a democratic basis. I think it is true to say that in the fifteen years which have elapsed since the above arrangements were made, neither party feels that mistakes have been made in the selection of overlookers.

IMPARTIAL COURTS OF JUSTICE

I now come to the third attribute of democracy—namely, that the people are protected against unjust administration of the laws by impartial Courts of Justice.

Some considerable time ago the directors came to the conclusion that in any cases of disputes which might arise between a worker and the management regarding any disciplinary action on the part of the latter, these should, in fairness, be settled not by the management, which was an interested party, but by an impartial person or persons. Under British law every one has a right to be tried by an impartial tribunal, and the directors decided that a similar right should be given to the workers in the Cocoa Works. They therefore arranged that wherever anyone had been subjected to disciplinary action for a breach of works rules, he could, if he felt aggrieved, appeal to an impartial court whose decision on the matter should be final. It was therefore proposed to the central works council that a court of this kind should be set up in the works, and a committee of workers and administrative officers was appointed to work out the details. The court, or, as it is known in the works, the Appeal Committee, consists of two persons elected by the workers, two nominated by the directors, with a chairman appointed jointly by the four. The members of this committee serve for a year and are eligible for re-election. Any worker who feels that disciplinary action taken against him for breach of a works rule, or for conduct not affecting the performance of his work, is unjust, may appeal to this committee, which may reverse a decision, reduce a penalty or increase it, and their decision is final. It may, and indeed on one occasion I remember it did, upset a decision made by the board of directors.

Appeals are not often made to the committee. In the seventeen years since it was appointed, up to June 1938, it has heard thirty-three cases. Two of these were not so much instances of an appeal, as occasions on which the committee was asked to adjudicate. Of the remaining thirty-one, fifteen were appeals against decisions of the theft committee.[1] In ten of these instances, its decision was upheld; in one case it was reversed; and in the remaining four instances the penalty was reduced. The remaining sixteen cases were appeals against decisions of the management; in seven of these the decisions were upheld; in six the committee decided in favour of the employee; and in the remaining three instances reduced the penalty inflicted.

Some of my fellow-employers, who have heard of this committee in our works, have asked whether we have not found it subversive of discipline. It is hard for them to realise that it can be wise for a board of directors to yield to a third party the right to the last word in disciplinary matters. When they raise this difficulty with me, I always tell them that in the long run authority depends upon justice. Before we had an appeal committee, if anyone thought he had been unjustly treated he could go round among his friends, both inside the works

[1] See p. 27.

and outside, spreading abroad an idea that he had been unjustly treated. But no man can do that to-day. If he opens his lips to make a complaint, people at once say to him, " If you are not satisfied, why don't you go to the Appeal Committee ? " It need not undermine the authority of the management to have a decision of theirs upset. I remember one occasion when a man came to see me because he had been dismissed for some serious breach of works rules, and he thought that his dismissal was unjust. After going carefully into the matter, I told him that I thought the decision was just and that I must uphold it, but I said to him, " All I want is justice. If you think you are being unjustly treated, go to the Appeal Committee, and if they reinstate you, I will be the first to congratulate you, for it is possible that my individual judgment may be wrong, and if it is I want it corrected." There is nothing to lower authority in taking up such a position.

THEFT COMMITTEE

In the case of theft, the procedure followed differs from that in connection with any other offence.

It will be readily understood that in a confectionery factory the temptation to steal is very great. In some factories employees are searched at uncertain intervals when leaving the works, but we have never adopted that method at the Cocoa Works. There always has been a good deal of pilfering, and by this I do not mean just the eating of chocolates while at work, but taking goods out of the factory. A great deal of thought was given to the question of how best this evil could be remedied, and the matter was discussed at length by the central council. Finally, it was arranged that a committee, now known as the " Theft Committee," should be set up. All cases of alleged theft of property belonging to the company, or committed on or about the company's premises at York, are, after preliminary investigation, referred to the theft committee, which takes any necessary action. This committee consists of six members, three elected by the worker members of the central council and three by the administrative members. The members meet as a body and elect a chairman from outside their number in whose impartiality all the members have confidence. The difference between this committee and the appeal committee is that in cases of suspected theft the only action which is taken by the management is to refer the matter to the theft committee. They themselves take no disciplinary action. If disciplinary action is taken by the theft committee, the worker against whom it is taken may appeal to the appeal committee. The number of cases brought before the theft committee in the last seventeen years has been 184, involving 259 persons, of whom 28 were found not guilty. Of the remainder 95 were dismissed and 136 suspended from work for varying periods.

The reason which led the directors to suggest to the central council that disciplinary action in connection with theft should be taken by an impartial committee, and not by the management, was that they hoped that this would lead to the creation of a public opinion throughout the works discouraging theft. Just as in a public school or in society, it is recognised that certain things " aren't done " by decent people, so it was hoped to create a spirit of public opinion against pilfering. I think it may be said that the appointment of the committee has met with a considerable measure of success in creating such a spirit, and no one wishes to revert to the old method of dealing with cases of theft. Reports by the committee are presented to the central council monthly, and the

annual report of the committee is made the occasion
for a careful review by the council of the policy
adopted by the committee. The interest of the
workers in the suppression of theft is intense, and on
several occasions a systematic survey of the many
opportunities for theft which exist in the factory
has been prepared for the council, and suggestions
made with a view to eliminating them. I am afraid
it has to be admitted that so long as sweets are sweet
and employees, especially young ones, are subject
to human frailty, a certain amount of petty thieving
will continue ! ! There are very few cases of serious
theft.

It may be asked why should not workers be able
to appeal to an impartial tribunal in the case of
disciplinary action no matter for what reason. For
instance, dismissal because they are unsatisfactory
workmen either through lack of skill, or on account
of laziness or other fault. I think it will be generally
agreed that the question of whether a workman is
or is not suitable for the work which he is asked to
do must rest with the employer. It is quite reasonable
that the worker should be protected against vindictive
action on the part of the employer, and later on I
describe the steps taken at the Cocoa Works to this
end, which go a long way towards safeguarding the
interests of the workers, but in these matters there is
no appeal against the decision of the management.

The rule which governs cases of this kind is as
follows :—

Any person feeling that injustice has been done
to him in connection with disciplinary action taken
against him under circumstances which do not
give him the right to go to the Appeal Committee,
has the right to appeal from the executive officer
with regard to whose action he complains, to the

executive officer immediately above him, and so on, if necessary, right up to the chairman of the York Board, whose decision shall be final. The chairman will give his decision after consultation with the director of the function concerned, the labour director, and the trade union representative or the employee making the appeal.

The fact that the chairman must consult with both parties to the dispute and with the labour director before giving his decision, reduces to an insignificant minimum any chance of his making a hasty and ill-considered decision.

FREEDOM OF SPEECH

We come now to the fourth attribute of democracy, namely, freedom of speech. This means in effect liberty to question the acts of the management. How far can such freedom be given in a factory without encouraging discontent ?

In the opinion of the directors at the Cocoa Works, if you want co-operation from the workers, they must be treated as partners in a common enterprise. You cannot expect to develop a spirit of true co-operation if the workers are refused the right to ask questions as to why certain things are done, and if they are not allowed to bring before the management criticism of any managerial policy with which they disagree. I remember, a long time ago, a foreman in the Cocoa Works (a very loyal and delightful man) saying to a worker who had suggested an improved method of carrying out a process, " Noo, lad, get on with tha' work. Thoo's paid to work—not to think." But that was fifty years ago, and a lot of water has flowed under London Bridge since then ! Yet I think there is still a tendency on the part of some employers to think it is unquestioningly their lot to command, and as unquestioningly the lot of the workers to obey, with no questions asked ; but a true spirit of co-operation will not come that way.

There is at the Cocoa Works great freedom to ask questions and to make criticisms. As already stated, at the departmental and central councils members may raise practically any questions they like, and it is found that no abuse results from this privilege. On the contrary, if there is a feeling among members of the council that in certain respects the action of the management is unwise or inefficient, it is far better that they should say so, for surely if they are right it is desirable that the matter should be dealt with, and if they are wrong it is important that this should be explained to them. People who are living under a sense that their efforts are being neutralised by mistakes or mismanagement on the part of others will not give of their best.

Acting on the principle that the workers have the right to know the full reasons for any acts of the management which directly concern them, it is considered important to keep nothing back from them when negotiating questions concerning wages. It will be remembered that basic wage rates are dealt with by the Interim Industrial Reconstruction Committee and apply to about forty per cent. of the workers in the confectionery industry, but any proposals with regard to wages above the basic rates, and negotiations in connection with any concession asked for by the workers as a whole from the management, or *vice versa*, are matters for discussion between the management and the local trade union. If ever we refuse any concession asked for or ask the workers to make a concession, we always put all the cards on the table. We show their representatives any relevant figures dealing with profits, and have never known them make improper use of the information given to them. We tell them they may ask any questions on the accounts they like, or if they think that the need to ask a concession from them is due to bad management they are at liberty to make any criticisms they like, or ask any questions. The directors consider that it would be improper for them to ask a concession from the workers, unless the financial position of the company at the moment justified such a course, nor would it be fair to ask them to accept the statement that the concession was necessary without offering them the opportunity of checking its accuracy.

It has for many years been our practice to keep the workers informed as to the trade position. This is done by the chairman of the York Board addressing the central council on the subject from time to time. In these addresses he informs the council about the sales in the different departments of the business, about any new goods which have been brought out or are contemplated, about special competition which the company has to meet, and any difficulties with which the company may at the moment be confronted. Sometimes samples are shown of goods offered by competitors at prices which we cannot match. It may be explained to the council that the competitor in question is paying wages very much lower than ours, and that his workers do not enjoy the various conditions, such as pension funds, holidays with pay, and so forth, which are enjoyed by the workers at the Cocoa Works ; and the workers are asked for any suggestions they may have as to ways in which we can lower the cost of production of our goods, so that they may be sold at competitive prices. Unless workers are kept informed with regard to matters of this kind, I do not see how they can possibly be expected to act in a co-operative spirit in seeking the success of the enterprise as a whole.

Once a year, immediately after the meeting of shareholders, the chairman gives a series of addresses in the works. He addresses a meeting of executive officers, the central council, and an open meeting of the workers. At these meetings he gives an account of the year's trading, dealing with the subject in much greater detail than would be suitable in a meeting of shareholders. He, naturally, treats the matter somewhat differently in the three meetings, in view of the different character of his audiences. After each meeting, opportunity is given for questions. The meetings of executives and the central council are held during works hours, but the open meeting is held in the evening. Any worker may attend this, and is at liberty to ask any question he likes, for questions are encouraged.

There is still another opportunity given to the workers to exercise the right of freedom of speech, and that is through a meeting of all shop stewards in the factory which is held once a year and attended by the chairman of the York Board of Directors. The chief shop steward presides over the meeting and explains that the chairman has come to answer any questions that any shop steward likes to ask. The chairman makes no speech ; he merely answers questions. When I was chairman of the York Board, I attended a number of these meetings, and the shop stewards were encouraged to ask any question or make any criticism they wished. It was an opportunity for the chairman to explain the why and wherefore of a great number of things that are done in the works, and sometimes he heard of matters which wanted putting right. I used to tell the shop stewards that if they would like to have meetings of this kind more frequently than once a year, I should be glad to attend, but an annual meeting seemed to meet their needs. My successor finds the meetings as useful as I did, and I know they are appreciated by the shop stewards.

Thus I think it may be said that there is almost complete freedom of speech in the works, and interchange of thought between the management and the workers. As a result there is less misunderstanding between them and a greater spirit of co-operation than if they lived in two different worlds.

THE SUGGESTION SCHEME

There is one further means by which employees may express their views and make suggestions with regard to matters connected with the factory. In common with many other employers we have instituted at the Cocoa Works a suggestion scheme which has been in operation for a great many years. Throughout the works in convenient places are locked " Suggestion Boxes." Any employee wishing to make a suggestion either in connection with technical processes, working conditions, administration or organisation, or any other matter connected with the works, may place particulars of his ideas on a form which he signs and places in one of these boxes. The suggestions are collected daily, copied (with the name deleted if the suggestor so requests), and distributed to the appropriate managers, who decide whether they should be adopted. The decision whether a prize should be given, and if so its amount, is in the hands of a committee representative of the management and the workers under the chairmanship of a director. Any employee whose suggestion is accepted is awarded a suitable money prize. But whether his suggestion is accepted or not, he is seen by his superior officer, thanked for his efforts and encouraged to continue them. No member of the management is directly rewarded for a suggestion, as he is expected to suggest improvement in methods and processes in the course of his ordinary duties. For a time the workers were somewhat chary of making suggestions, as they felt that their immediate superiors might regard them as reflecting on their own ability to visualise possible improvements. This feeling has, however, been dissipated, and it is now generally regarded as creditable to an overlooker to have under him employees who are interested and keen enough to think out improvements. 621 suggestions were made under this scheme during 1937, and 192 prizes varying in amount up to £25 awarded. In certain cases where it is difficult to assess the ultimate value of a suggestion, a later review is made and the original award increased if warranted. To encourage initiative, special awards are sometimes made in cases where exceptional thought or labour has been expended on a suggestion—even though it may not have been adopted.

Shop Stewards

I think, perhaps, the present will be the most convenient place in which to say something about the part which shop stewards play in the Cocoa Works.[1] The manual workers are represented by a total of forty-five shop stewards ; the clerks by fourteen, and the allied engineering trades by five. These shop stewards form an important link between the workers and the management ; indeed, I think it is no exaggeration to say that in the day-to-day management of a department, no matter of any importance which directly affects the workers is settled without discussing it with them. For instance, if short time or overtime is to be worked, the shop steward is informed before

[1] For a statement of the duties of shop stewards, see footnote, p. 11.

C

the order is given, and he has an opportunity of saying anything he wishes about it. If it is necessary to reduce the staff in a department, either temporarily or permanently, the management submits to the shop steward for his information and approval the names of those with whose services it is proposed to dispense. In the rare event of non-agreement, each case is further considered by the management and shop steward, in conjunction with the employment department, with whom the final decision rests.

This consultation with the shop steward gives to workers a sense of security against any unfair action on the part of the management. No man can complain that he has been dismissed " because the foreman has got his knife into him " !

There is another step which has been taken in connection with the shop stewards which has had far-reaching effects. In 1920, the directors offered the chairman of the local branch of the National Union of General and Municipal Workers, who was working in one of the production departments, a post in the labour department, with the title of Chief Shop Steward. They recognised that the suggestion that the local chairman of the union should enter the labour department was one on which the union might look with considerable suspicion, thinking that the directors wanted to put him in a position in which he would be strongly influenced by the opinions of the management. However, the matter was frankly discussed with the union and in the central works council. It was explained that the object with which the proposal to appoint a representative of the workers on the staff of the labour department was being made would be defeated if he ceased accurately to reflect the opinion of the workers in connection with any subject under discussion. The fact that in the eighteen years which have elapsed since he joined the labour department he has never failed to be elected annually as the chairman of the local branch of the union proves that he has not lost their confidence.

If any difficulty arises in a department which the departmental shop steward fails to settle, he refers it to the chief shop steward. In addition to this, individual workers frequently bring complaints to him about anything with which they are dissatisfied. If, as often happens, these are not justified but are due to ignorance of why certain things are done or not done, he is able to explain this to the worker, who will more readily accept an explanation if given by the chairman of his union than if it were given to him by the management. On the other hand, if the chief shop steward finds that a complaint is justified, he either advises the worker as to the step he should take to have it dealt with, or he may take up the matter himself with the administrative officer concerned. As chief shop steward, he has the right to discuss matters with any administrative officer in the factory, and if he does not get satisfaction, he can, if necessary, take it right up to the chairman of the York Board. But, as a matter of fact, matters are almost invariably settled promptly in a friendly way long before such a stage is reached. Indeed, during sixteen years when I was chairman of the York Board, I can only remember one complaint made by a worker which the chief shop steward was obliged to bring to me for settlement.

Obviously, his position is not an easy one. He has to retain the confidence both of the workers and the management. If he failed to put the workers' case with adequate force, they would feel he was not serving them loyally. If, on the other hand, he were to look at every question only from the workers' standpoint, then the management might regard him as being prejudiced. He has, however, succeeded in winning the confidence of both management and men, and the appointment has been amply justified by results.

SUMMARY AND CONCLUSIONS

Before passing to other questions, let us seek to measure the real significance of the facts reported on in this chapter.

We have seen how the working rules of the factory have been made with, and cannot be altered without, the agreement of the workers ; that foremen are not appointed except after consultation with the workers, and that it has been found possible always to reach agreement with regard to the appointments made. Workers are protected against mal-administration of the works rules by impartial courts of justice, and in those cases of disciplinary action regarding which they cannot appeal to these courts, they have the right, either directly or through their trade union representative, to bring the matter before the chairman of the York Board, if they cannot get it settled elsewhere in the organisation. Although his decision is final, it can only be given after consultation with the director of the function concerned, the labour director and the employee making the appeal. If the employee wishes he may be represented by an official of his union.

In addition to the above, the workers enjoy wide freedom to express their views upon managerial acts and policy, and to obtain information as to why things are either done or not done.

It will, I think, be agreed that employees working under these conditions are treated as co-operators and not as factory " hands."

It may, however, be said that so long as they are not represented on the board of directors, the measure of co-operation accorded to them falls short of that which they might reasonably expect. We have not adopted this course at the Cocoa Works, since it entails certain definite disadvantages. If, on the one hand, worker directors were appointed for a short time only, they would be handicapped at the directors' meetings, where long experience of the business, with its many problems, is essential to taking part usefully in the discussions. On the other hand, if, once appointed, they practically remained on the board for life, they would tend to get out of touch with their fellow-workers, and the purpose for which they had been elected would not be fulfilled. But to say this is not to say that the door to the board room is closed to workers of any grade or class. On the contrary, directors are chosen solely on account of their ability to manage the business skilfully; whenever there is a vacancy on the board it is filled by the man who is thought to be best qualified to fill it. Thus no worker is prevented from becoming a director if he possesses the necessary qualifications; indeed, three members of the present board entered the service of the company as junior clerks at a few shillings a week, while a fourth, who entered the service as a weekly wage earner in the engineering department, became chairman of the York Board and is now vice-chairman of the company. In the opinion of the directors, it would be opposed to the interests of the business, and therefore to those of the workers, to add to the board any directors other than the ablest men they can find.

I can imagine that some business executives reading this chapter may imagine that our method of doing things must lead to much delay, but that is not the case. In all matters of day-to-day management where conference is desired, it takes place informally between the executive officer concerned and the shop steward. The decisions of councils and committees are almost exclusively concerned with broad questions where a little delay doesn't matter. If any matter arises which affects the central council and which must be dealt with urgently, it is referred to the executive committee of the council, which is a small body and can be summoned quickly.

Reviewing the whole question of the status of the workers in the Cocoa Works, I cannot think that they would enjoy a higher status if industry were conducted on socialistic or communistic principles. In coming to this conclusion, I bear in mind the fact that in the interests of the workers the business must be conducted efficiently, and that this fact places definite limitations upon the degree of liberty which individual workers can enjoy. I do not, of course, suggest that our methods of dealing with the matters discussed in this chapter are ideal—indeed, I hope it may be found possible to improve them as greatly in the next fifteen years, as we have been able to do in the last fifteen ; but meanwhile they are working well. When any question affecting the workers arises, it is approached by the workers and the management, not as opposing forces, but as partners in a joint enterprise, the success of which is a matter of importance to both of them.

CHAPTER II

WAGES

WE now leave the question of the workers' status and turn to consider their remuneration. It is fitting that an early chapter of a book on the human side of business administration should treat of wages, for an industry which does not pay minimum wages which will at any rate enable the workers to live in reasonable comfort fails in one of its chief duties to the community. Of course, an individual employer cannot determine the wages in his factory without regard to those paid by his competitors, but this does not absolve him from all responsibility in the matter. If the wages current in his industry are inadequate to enable the lowest paid workers to live in moderate comfort, there are two things he should do. First, he should try to persuade his Employers' Federation to take steps to have a Trade Board set up in the industry, which would protect " good " employers from the competition of those content to pay sweated wages; and second, so far as economic conditions allow, he should seek to pay reasonable wages to the lowest paid workers in his own factory, irrespective of what others are paying.

WHAT ARE " REASONABLE WAGES " ?

But what are " reasonable wages " ? In the case of a man, I think they may be defined as wages sufficient to allow him to marry, to live in a decent house, and to maintain a family of normal size (generally taken as consisting of five persons) in physical efficiency, with a moderate margin for contingencies and recreation.   In the case of a woman, who, as a rule, has not to maintain dependants, the minimum wage should enable her to live comfortably in respectable surroundings with a margin for incidental expenses.

An estimate of the wages necessary to live in accord with these standards is given, along with the basis on which it was founded, in my book *The Human Needs of Labour*.[1] With the cost of living as it was in 1936, I gave 53s. for men in towns and 41s. 6d. in the country as being the lowest minimum wages which could be defended.[2] The minimum for women was 30s. 9d.   These figures will, of course, fluctuate with the cost of living, and so no permanent figure can be stated, but there is no doubt that the wages normally received by unskilled labourers often fall short of the necessary sum.

Can Industry afford Higher Real Wages for Low-Paid Workers ?

It is true that, in many cases, to raise minimum wages to-morrow by a substantial amount would be impossible, since industry could not adapt itself to so sudden a change. But I suggest that all employers should definitely set before them, as an end to be achieved with the least possible delay, the payment of such wages as will allow their lowest paid workers to live in health and reasonable comfort.   It is a mistake for them to leave all the pressure in connection with wage advances to be made by the

[1] *Human Needs of Labour.* Longmans, Green & Co., London. Second and revised edition, 2s. 6d.

[2] In these estimates 9s. 6d. is allowed for rent and rates in towns, and 5s. 6d. in the country.

workers. Of course, there are already many employers who are not in favour of low-paid labour, and who pay all they can, but this should be the policy not only of individuals, but of employers as a class. The adoption of such an attitude would revolutionise industrial relations, and do much to allay labour unrest.

There is no single specific which will render generally possible the payment of adequate minimum wages. The desired end may be achieved by adopting one of three courses, or, more often, by adopting more than one of these at the same time. The three courses are to increase selling prices, to reduce profits, and to reduce costs.

The first method tends to defeat its own end, for it raises the cost of living, and thus lowers the value of wages. It is justified, however, when selling prices in a particular industry are too low in relation to other costs and services produced in comparable conditions of efficiency. In such circumstances there is a case for joint effort by the different employers in the industry to raise wages. With regard to the second, the only fund available is the " surplus profits," *i.e.* profits over and above what are necessary to keep the business financially sound. Of course there are industries which habitually make surplus profits, but I think that unprejudiced persons will agree that the problem of how to raise real wages cannot be solved merely by reducing profits. Turning now to the third method, the wealth produced per worker depends partly on his own exertions and partly on those of others. So far as his own exertions are concerned, there is no doubt that they represent a potential source of increased wealth, which varies greatly from worker to worker and from trade to trade. Many workers are not doing their best, and will tell you so quite frankly. It is the task of those who are responsible for the administration of industry on its human side to seek out the causes for this, and to find appropriate remedies. I refer to this question frequently in succeeding chapters, and will only say here that the causes are often deep-rooted. Among them are the fear of " working oneself out of a job," the risk of rate-cutting in the case of piece-workers, and the belief that no advantage will accrue to the worker as a result of increased effort.

Turning to the possibility of increasing the production of wealth by means other than the exertion of the wage-earners, it will not be disputed that many factories are still running on inefficient lines. Much of the machinery is antiquated, the buildings are badly planned, the staff and workers are ill-trained, and the work badly organised. In such cases the profits earned are often inconsiderable, even when wages are low, and any request for higher wages is met by the argument that the industry cannot afford them. What is here needed is a critical examination of each process, and of the organisation of the factory as a whole to see whether the profit margin can be increased. Only after a minute examination, on these lines, is an employer really in a position to say whether his industry can or cannot afford to pay higher wages. I suggest that the aim of every employer should be to provide equipment and organisation which will enable every worker to earn good wages, and to establish a relationship with the workers which will encourage each of them to take the fullest advantage of these opportunities. I have not been a lifetime in business without realising how difficult this is, but if experience has made me conscious of the difficulty, it has also impressed on me the importance of overcoming it, and has strengthened my belief that it is possible to do so. I must refer the reader to other books for a discussion of methods of business efficiency. The matter is only mentioned here because I want to press home the fact that failure to render a business thoroughly efficient injures not only the shareholders but the workers.

At the Cocoa Works, considerable benefit has resulted from the activities of a body known as the "Research Committee." It consists of engineers, chemists, and cost-accountants, who, in association with the managers and others in the departments concerned, systematically overhaul the processes employed in the factory. They take nothing for granted, but examine every process in the light of the best scientific and technical knowledge available. Although the expense involved is considerable, it is amply justified by the results obtained.

THE ORGANISATION OF A WAGES SECTION

I pass now to the question of the organisation to be set up to deal specifically with wages—in other words, from the material to the human side of the wages problem. The first step is to make someone in the factory responsible for supervising all questions of wages. These are so important and their co-ordination so necessary that they cannot be allowed to take their chance at the hands of a number of different officials. In a small factory, one of the principals should accept responsibility for this side of the business administration, delegating details to someone directly responsible to himself. In a large factory the work will be carried out by an executive occupying a position of authority.

Assuming that the utmost is being done to provide efficient administration and equipment, the duty of this executive is to see that every worker is encouraged to take the fullest advantage of the oppor-

tunity thus provided to earn high wages. I here
emphasise the word *earn*.

This will involve—

(1) In the case of workers paid " on day," the
constant adjustment of wages (within permissible
limits) to the value of the service rendered.

(2) In the case of workers who are paid by results,
the development of just and equitable systems
of payment which will most effectively encourage
them to do their best.

In all this work, I would emphasise the fundamental
importance of insisting on " the fair deal." Only
thus can an atmosphere in which the workers do their
best be created and maintained. This necessitates—

(3) Organisation which provides for dealing
promptly with all questions raised affecting the
earnings of an individual or a group of workers.

The last point is important, for much labour
unrest to-day is caused by delay in settling grievances
which may individually seem unimportant to the
management, and which are capable of easy solution,
but which, if allowed to accumulate, create a widespread sense of discontent. It cannot be too clearly
remembered that although the employer is apt to
regard his wage bill as a whole, and to consider it
primarily in relation to his cost of production and his
balance-sheet, to the worker the wage received at
the week-end is an exceedingly individual matter.
It is small comfort to an employee who, from one
cause or another, receives less than the sum to which
he considers himself entitled, to know that *on the
average* the wages paid in his department are adequate.
To a man who is living on the margin, a shilling or
two below his usual wage means running into debt,

or going without some necessary, while a shilling or two more may mean the power to secure something which makes a real difference to the joy of life.

A wise management will not only regard wages as a whole, but consider their relation to every individual worker. In saying this, I do not, of course, lose sight of the fact that in certain industries there is no system of payment by results. Moreover, some trade unions still insist on the payment of a flat rate to every one in each particular grade, independently of individual worth. But such a system has a deadening effect, and the tendency of industry is to depart from it. An increasing proportion of trade unions accept payment by results, and even when that is not the case, many trade agreements, while laying down minimum wages, allow for the recognition of individual merit or responsibility.

Before describing the methods adopted at the Cocoa Works for dealing with wages, it should be stated how the minimum wages in the Cocoa and Confectionery industries are fixed. Since 1913 minimum wages have been fixed by a Trade Board, but these represent the absolute minimum which must be paid by every one engaged in the industry, and are substantially lower than the wages currently paid by some of the larger firms. In 1918 an Interim Industrial Reconstruction Committee[1] was formed, and a materially higher scale of minimum wages and certain other conditions, such as holidays with pay, special payment

[1] The functions performed by Interim Industrial Reconstruction Committees are practically the same as those performed by Joint Industrial, or " Whitley " Councils—but the latter are only recognised by the Minister of Labour when set up in industries where both employers and workers are highly organised. In less highly organised industries an Interim Industrial Reconstruction Committee takes the place of the Joint Industrial Council. It is not regarded by the Minister of Labour as speaking with quite so authoritative a voice on trade questions as a Joint Industrial Council.

for shift work, etc., were agreed upon between the representatives of employers and the trade unions on that committee. Membership of the committee is voluntary. About twelve firms, employing about forty per cent. of the workers in the industry, are members of the committee and carry out the conditions agreed upon.[1] The trade unions who are parties to the wage agreement have undertaken not to approach individually, with a view to securing an increase in the basic wage rate, any firm which, like our own, is a party to the agreement made by the above committee. These conditions only apply to workers directly concerned with the manufacture of cocoa, chocolate and confectionery. They do not apply to members of the maintenance staff, such as joiners or builders, nor to clerks. Minimum wages are fixed solely according to age ; no attempt is made in the agreement to assess the value of services above the minimum. Piece rates must be so fixed as to enable workers of average ability to earn at least twenty-five per cent. above the time-rate.

It is a great step in advance to have such a minimum wage fixed for so large a proportion of the workers in the industry ; but it is only an initial step. An enormous amount of detailed work on wages is left to each individual firm. Arrangements must be made as to the relative value of all kinds of services worth more than a minimum wage, and piece rates or other forms of payment by results must be established wherever possible, which will yield to the average worker at least the minimum laid down in the agreement.

[1] When this book was first published in 1921 the figure was seventy-five per cent., but since 1921 a number of employers, feeling the effects of trade depression, have withdrawn from the group of those who agree to be bound by the decisions of the Interim Industrial Reconstruction Committee, so that now (1938), as stated, only about forty per cent. of the workers in the industry are directly affected by them.

Until 1919, each department in the Cocoa Works was responsible for dealing with its own wages, and working out its own piece rates. In spite of quarterly reviews of wages by an inter-departmental committee, it was found that there were great variations in the way in which wage problems were dealt with in different departments, and this gave rise to considerable dissatisfaction in departments which were less liberally treated than others. After the war, therefore, machinery was introduced to secure more perfect co-ordination throughout the factory, in the matter of wages. A Wages Section was established, and was made responsible for the wage policy of the whole factory. In view of the importance of the wage question, it may be worth while to explain the system we have adopted, and the duties of the Wages Section, in some little detail.[1] The objects for which it was established are as follows :—

(1) To ensure complete co-ordination in the methods of dealing with wages throughout the factory.

(2) To set up machinery necessary for keeping a constant survey of the wages of every worker, and advising the departments concerned whenever a wage appears to be anomalous, so that inquiry may be made as to the cause of this.

(3) To ensure that the provisions and requirements of the Sugar Confectionery and other Trade Boards applicable to sections of the works, and of the Interim Industrial Reconstruction Committee, are scrupulously observed.

(4) To give expert advice to the departments

[1] The wages section forms part of the labour department, which is under the control of the labour director and labour manager. Details of the work undertaken by the labour department are given on p. 99 *et seq.*

on the best method of payment by result to adopt in any particular case.

(5) To obtain, and keep up to date, full infor- mation regarding rates and wages paid throughout the country for every kind of service rendered by workers employed at the Cocoa Works. Two purposes are served by this comprehensive survey of current wages. First, where we find that our wages are falling behind the national standard, we can rectify the matter before a complaint reaches us, and thus prevent dissatisfaction ; and second, when an application for an advance in wages is made, we are in a position to see how far this is justified, in relation to the national standard.

(6) To obtain, and keep up to date, information relating to methods of remuneration adopted else- where.

(7) To negotiate with trade unions on all questions affecting wages.[1] Where these concern workers in one department only, this task is usually under- taken in conjunction with the manager of the department concerned.

It will be seen that if the above scheme is working efficiently, it provides so detailed a knowledge of the wages earned week by week by every one through- out the factory, and of the wages paid for similar services elsewhere, that legitimate causes of complaint should not arise. Whenever the wages of an individual worker are seen to be abnormal, the department con-

---

[1] Although the Interim Industrial Reconstruction Committee fixes the basic wage scales, questions affecting individuals or groups of workers arise from time to time which are either settled with the workers, or by negotiation with the local branch of the trade union. Besides, there are, as stated, a number of workers with whose wages the Interim Industrial Reconstruction Committee is not concerned.

cerned is made aware of it, and the matter dealt with. It is not suggested that the work now being done by the wages section was never done before. Most of it had been done from the outset by separate departments, but it is now more thoroughly co-ordinated, and is no longer just one item in the heavy burden falling upon departmental managers, an item which may sometimes be squeezed out on account of the pressure of other very urgent work.

TIME STUDY AND THE WAGES SECTION

When setting piece or bonus rates, the amount of output which can fairly be asked in return for standard wages is, of course, a matter of fundamental importance. In the old days it had been the custom at the Cocoa Works to fix this by rule of thumb methods. However, in 1922 we decided that the time had come to introduce more reliable methods of fixing standard outputs. We discussed the matter fully with the trade union, and with its full approval every job in the factory is now time studied. The close co-operation with the trade union when time study was first introduced, and the fact that full opportunity is always given to the workers' representatives to satisfy themselves that the time studies are carried out under conditions which are fair to all concerned, have resulted in their being accepted by the workers without resentment. They are now regarded as a perfectly normal item of works routine.

On the basis of their average earnings the workers to be time studied are selected by the management and their names notified to the shop steward, who must be satisfied that, in all respects, they are workers of average ability. When the study is completed, a statement of the piece rate to be paid is drawn up and signed by the manager of the department, the

D

shop steward, and the time study assistant. They also agree upon and sign a statement of the exact conditions under which the test was made. This is important, because if, in practice, these conditions are not fulfilled and the workers' output suffers in consequence, the firm undertakes to make good any loss which they may sustain. The work of making time studies is undertaken by a specially trained staff, one or more of whom is attached to a department, and they thus become familiar with the processes which they have to time study. In some departments workers have, at their own request, been trained to take time study observations, and from time to time are asked to help in this work ; no objection is raised when they time study their fellow-workers. The whole of the work connected with time study is under the direction of a trained time and motion study manager, who co-ordinates the work done in different departments.

By reason of the care and attention given to the question of standard output, the fixing of the rate which will yield standard earnings has become merely a nominal duty of the wages section. More important, however, is the duty of dealing with situations in which the conditions under which the time study was made have been departed from. As stated above, any loss due to this cause for which the workers are not to blame, entails a payment to them in compensation for loss of earnings. The amount of such compensation is settled by the departmental manager, acting on the advice of the time study manager and the wages section.

An incidental advantage of fixing standard outputs in the way just described is that improved methods of doing the work are constantly being suggested by the men who are engaged in taking time studies. This is not unnatural, for they are, as it were, putting each job under a microscope and studying each individual movement. On completion of a study definite methods of operation are selected, and these are demonstrated to the workers by teachers and trainers attached to the various departments.

GUARANTEE OF PIECE RATES

One of the most serious criticisms which workers, as a rule, make of piece-work is that if they work very hard in order to earn good wages, the piece rates are liable to be cut. They regard this as grossly unjust, and often refrain from doing their best.

Some time ago we felt at the Cocoa Works that steps should, if possible, be taken to remove from the minds of the workers any fear that rates would be reduced unless a mistake had quite definitely been made in fixing them, or unless changes in the processes involved had occurred which affected the effort necessary to produce a given output. After discussing the matter with the workers' representatives, the following was agreed to between the management and the workers, and now finds a place among the list of rules agreed to by the central council :—

Existing rates (standard of output) will not be altered unless it is agreed with the workers' representatives that a change affecting the rate of output attainable for the same effort has taken place in—

(1) Machine or other equipment.
(2) Material used.
(3) Process or method of manufacture, or
(4) Other conditions.

Wherever it is agreed that a mistake has been made in the setting of a rate, correction will be made without delay.

Subject to what has been said above, the company guarantee that the standard output required to earn standard piece or bonus money will remain unaltered except as provided above, and that standard outputs on new jobs (including all existing jobs for which the final rate has not yet been set) will be similarly guaranteed when sufficient time and practice have been allowed for attaining normal skill on the job.

This rule has now been in operation for a number of years, and no difficulty has been found in agreeing with the workers about any change which either they or the management considered necessary.

When fixing the standard output of a new job, it is not always easy to say when a group of workers has been working on the job long enough to reach its normal output, with the result that a rate may be set either too tight or too loose. If it is too tight, the workers will certainly approach the management with a view to having it raised, and it is, therefore, only fair that if it is too loose, the management should have the right to approach the workers with a view to having it lowered. Both sides recognise that it is difficult to set piece rates on new jobs, and in all negotiations both parties have sought to arrive at a fair wage. The same is true when changes of wages are called for owing to alterations which have occurred in connection with the processes concerned. I think it may be said that the close co-operation and the mutual confidence which have been established between management and labour have been of advantage to both parties and have removed the fear of rate-cutting from the minds of the workers.

It is obvious that the greatest services of a central wages section are rendered in connection with piece-work, but it is also of considerable use in determining the remuneration of day workers. As already stated, the minimum wages are fixed by the Interim Industrial Reconstruction Committee. But these are flat rates varying only with the worker's age ; any wages above the minimum must be fixed by each factory separately. To secure uniformity of treatment, all day workers are divided into grades, four in the case of men, and three in the case of women, according to the work on which they are engaged. The wages payable in each grade vary within a limit of three or four shillings a week, according to the individual merit or responsibility of the workers, and the lowest of the grades begins at the minimum wage fixed by the Interim Industrial Reconstruction Committee. In fixing the rate of jobs above minimum, the co-operation of the workers is obtained through a grading committee. On this the chief shop steward and the shop steward of the section where the job is to be graded act with the labour manager or his deputy and the departmental manager. They visit the job and, in light of certain agreed definitions of grades and scales of pay, decide what the job is to be paid. No day wage is fixed without first notifying the wages section, which is responsible for advising the departmental manager concerned whether the proposed alteration is in conformity with the policy of the factory as a whole. Of course, it does not presume to dictate to a departmental manager whether John Smith, working in a particular grade, should be paid the minimum or the maximum wage of that grade. But it does advise him whether, generally speaking, he is adopting a similar policy to that adopted by other managers in assessing the value of his workers. Apart from such help, it might easily happen that in one department most of the men were paid the maximum for the grade, while in another most of them received the minimum.

The Workers' Share in Profits

Whilst we have for many years (as will appear from other portions of this book) utilised profits for the benefit of employees in different ways, we did not adopt a formal profit-sharing scheme until 1923. I had myself on more than one occasion gone into the matter (somewhat superficially), but had always come to the conclusion that profit-sharing, apparently, had not been very successful, and that in the light of the experience of others, it would be wiser not to adopt any formal scheme. However, I came increasingly to feel that in a completely satisfactory industrial structure the workers of all grades should have a definite share in the prosperity of the business in which they were engaged. As a result of this, in 1919 and 1920 I had an elaborate investigation made into profit-sharing. Particulars were obtained regarding about 329 profit-sharing schemes commenced in Great Britain and Ireland. I cannot here go into any great detail with regard to this investigation, but I think it desirable to give briefly the main conclusions.

In the first place, practical experience bore out the conclusion suggested by theory, that if what is wanted is primarily some method or device which will tend to stimulate the worker to greater effort day by day, some system of payment by results is likely to be much more effective than any true scheme of profit-sharing. The essentials for any satisfactory scheme of payment by results are—

(1) that the method of calculation should be simple, and easily understood ;

(2) that the payment should follow immediately or soon after the effort ; and

(3) that the reward should bear a direct relation to the effort.

Profit-sharing, as a rule, satisfies none of these tests. It does undoubtedly constitute some financial incentive in the direction desired, and may be worth adopting when other systems of payment by results are excluded for any reason, such as the nature of the business, or trade union opposition, but as a mere financial inducement to individual effort its direct effect is not likely to be great, and if this is the primary object in view the aim should be to introduce a suitable system of payment by results. One must not, however, on this account assume that profit-sharing is not worth while. On the contrary, the investigations convinced me that the chances of success for a profit-sharing scheme, properly devised and administered, were much greater than was generally thought.[1]

Having arrived at the above view, the board decided to adopt the principle of profit-sharing, and to put it into force at the Cocoa Works. I think the precise procedure adopted in doing so may be of interest to other employers. The first step was to appoint a small committee to consider the main lines of a proposed scheme and to determine what should be the extent of the offer to employees. When these proposals had reached a proper form, they were submitted to the central council, which was asked to elect five representatives, who would join with five representatives nominated by the board in the formulation of a complete scheme to be presented to the board and to the central council. Of the workers' representatives, one was elected by the managers, one by the overlookers, and three by the representatives of the remaining workers on the central council. The committee's recommendations were unanimous, with the exception of two reservations made by one

---

[1] A more detailed summary of the results of the above-named investigation into profit-sharing is given in Appendix I, p. 190 *et seq.*

member. The scheme was finally approved by the central council, after considerable debate ; and after receiving the approval of the directors, was then submitted to the two trade unions covering the great majority of our employees, for consideration from the point of view of trade union interests. Again, after considerable discussion, the approval of the unions was notified. I have laid stress on these steps because it is important that there should be the fullest consultation with both one's own employees and with the trade unions chiefly concerned, before the introduction of such a scheme, if it is to meet with general acceptance. The " take-it-or-leave-it " attitude will destroy practically the whole value of a profit-sharing scheme in advance.

Briefly, the scheme is this. We begin with a wage to labour and to capital. Labour's wage consists of the wages or salaries which would be paid if there were no profit-sharing scheme at all. Our whole proposals are founded on the principle that our wage rates shall be at least up to trade union standards. Otherwise, there would usually be no sound foundation on which a profit-sharing scheme could be based. There would be no guarantee that what was being paid to the workers as their share of profits was not being found in whole or in part as a result of the payment of lower wages. Capital's wage consists of a cumulative wage of seven and a half per cent. on " capital." This is approximately one per cent. in excess of the average dividend on our preference shares. The wage being cumulative, any arrears are carried forward and paid up in future years, which is just the same as would be done in the case of unpaid wages due to a worker. " Capital " for the purposes of the scheme consists of the issued share capital, together with the reserves and carry-forward standing in the books at the date when the scheme was intro-

duced, increased or reduced in the future according
as new capital is brought in, or reserves are paid out.
It may be mentioned that the figure taken as capital
in this way is substantially less than the market value
of the business, especially as our balance sheet includes
no item of goodwill.

After labour and capital have received their wage,
certain reserves are made. In the first place, each
year, when the profits available after providing for
capital's wage permit of this, there is set aside, either
£20,000 or ten per cent. of the profits remaining after
providing capital's wage for the year, whichever
is the greater. This is placed to a Dividends Equal-
isation Reserve, and is available for making up the
wage of capital in bad years. This reserve is not to
exceed in the aggregate one year's wage of capital.
Secondly, thereafter, the directors may set aside such
sum as they think fit to advertising reserve. This
reserve again, however, is not to exceed in the aggregate ten per cent. on capital without the consent of
the profit-sharing committee.[1] Finally, there is
power to set aside sums to a special reserve to meet
special circumstances, of which the Great War is an
example. An important point to be noted is that
(with one possible minor qualification justified by the
circumstances) all these reserves are ultimately brought
back into the pool and distributed under the terms
of the scheme. The setting aside of sums in this way
does not therefore in the end deprive labour of any
share of profits which it would otherwise have taken.
Several schemes have foundered upon this rock.

After providing for capital's wage and these reserves,
one-half of any remaining profits is set aside as
labour's share, one-tenth as the share of direction,
and the remaining four-tenths as the extra share of
capital. Labour's share is divided amongst all employ-

[1] See p. 59.

ees over sixteen who have been continuously employed
for not less than eight complete consecutive quarters.
In the case of weekly wage earners the regulations
provide for distribution in proportion to the forty-four
hour pick-up of the individual over the year. The
share is normally paid into a bank, but may be withdrawn at the employee's option. There is power in
certain circumstances, however, to pay labour's portion in the form of shares.

Direction's share is taken by the board of directors
in addition to their normal remuneration. In this
connection there is a provision, which I believe to
be unique, to the effect that if in any year the total
salaries of directors exceed the total at the date
when the scheme was introduced, the profit-sharing
committee may ask for information as to the amount
of the excess and if they regard it as unreasonable,
after taking into account the amount of the company's
business and the directors' duties, they may require
the question to be submitted to arbitration ; if any
portion is disallowed, this will be deducted from the
directors' share of profits. Broadly speaking, the
profits for the purposes of the scheme are profits for
the purposes of Income Tax.

Special consideration was throughout given to the
trade union position. For example, provisions have
been inserted in the scheme that a lock-out or an
authorised strike is not to be considered as a breach
in service, leading to forfeiture of the right to profits
under the scheme. Again, one of the regulations
is to the effect that it is the desire of the company
that the scheme shall not alter the position of trade
unionism at the works, that it is desirable in the
interests of the company and its employees that the
latter shall be suitably organised, and that membership of a trade union is, in the generality of cases,
desirable. There is a profit-sharing committee of

nine members, eight of whom are elected by the central
council and one by the outside staff. The committee
has substantial powers ; including among other things
the right to appoint an employees' accountant to
certify that the annual statement prepared under
the scheme by the company's auditors is correct.
This right has never been exercised. Here again
there is a power to go to arbitration in the event of
dispute.

The reception given to the scheme may be indicated
by reference to a memorandum from the central
council to all employees (signed by the worker chairman of the council), which includes the following
statements amongst others :—

"We believe that the directors introduced this
scheme as part of a carefully considered policy by
which they have sought to give to the workers
a greater share in the prosperity of the undertaking,
and to establish a more satisfactory relationship
between employer and employed. . . . We believe
this new bond between the company and its employees will lead to closer co-operation, for the latter
are now in an important sense partners. They
have a more direct common interest in the securing
of profits, since they share half and half in any
surplus. We believe that it is clearly in the interests
of all of us, whether our work is operative, technical,
or administrative, to make the business as successful
as may be. The best safeguard in the long run
against unemployment and short time will be found
in the closer co-operation that will result from
this common interest. . . ."

"We desire to express our appreciation of the
scheme and the motives which prompted it. At the
moment profits may be small (though consideration
of the scheme was begun when profits were high),

but we may hope for a steady improvement. In any case, we have the knowledge that whenever there are surplus profits we shall get a substantial share. We are now working in a sense on our own account."

There have been only two distributions under the scheme since its inauguration. In 1929 this amounted to two per cent., and in 1936 to two and a half per cent. on the wages and salaries bill. In this connection it should be remembered that the wage of capital is cumulative ; arrears have to be met out of surplus profits before a distribution is made.

The question may well be asked whether the fact that profits have only been distributed twice in fourteen years has given rise to dissatisfaction among the workers. I think the answer is that it has caused disappointment, but not dissatisfaction. Twice a year when the company balance sheet is got out, the chairman of the York board of directors makes a detailed statement to the profit-sharing committee with regard to the profits which have been earned, and the different factors which have affected the profit position. He explains just what steps the directors have taken and are taking to render the business as profitable as may be, and he answers any questions put to him. A report of this meeting, in summary form, is presented to the central council, and their representatives inform the workers that they have satisfied themselves that the reason why there has been no distribution of profits has been that there were no surplus profits to distribute, and that nothing is being held back from the workers which is their due. If there had been no profit-sharing scheme, the machinery would not have existed which would have enabled the directors to convince the workers as a body that they were getting a fair share of the profits earned by the business. One factor which lessened the sense of disappointment on the part of the workers is, of course, that the period covered included years of intense trade depression when profits were not easy to come by. I think, too, that they understand that the policy of the directors always has been to pay the workers the highest wage and to give them the best working conditions in the way of pension schemes, unemployment funds, medical services, and so forth that the business could afford. It would have been easy to distribute substantial surplus profits year by year had the directors followed a policy of paying the lowest wages which would enable them to obtain the necessary labour and avoiding all expenditure for such services as those just referred to.

CHAPTER III

ECONOMIC SECURITY

It is coming to be generally realised that something must be done to render the economic position of manual workers less insecure. Although an appreciable number of them are in situations which hold out every prospect of permanency, the majority have constantly hovering over them a cloud of uncertainty with regard to their future. At any time they may be discharged at a week's, or possibly an hour's, notice, and since any reserve they have laid up is probably slender, they are likely, if their unemployment continues for long, to experience serious privation. Even those who escape this tragedy will often find themselves in very straitened circumstances if they live to old age. Unless he is a highly paid worker, a man who has had to bring up three or four children cannot save enough to make adequate provision for his old age.

Again, there is always before working people the risk of being reduced to abject want through chronic invalidity. There are few more pathetic sights than that of a young, keen workman stricken down in early life with a disease which, although not mortal, prevents him from working.

Although the various measures of social insurance now provided for by law are on a scale more liberal than in any other country, they are obviously inadequate to free workers from anxiety, nor are the earnings of the workers sufficient, if each acts independently, to enable them to safeguard themselves against the above contingencies. Some organised effort is required to guarantee to the workers and their families a greater degree of economic security than they at present enjoy. In this chapter I propose to describe the steps taken at the Cocoa Works to achieve this end.

I shall deal with the matter under four heads :—

Unemployment.
Sickness.
Chronic Invalidity.
Old Age and Death.

UNEMPLOYMENT

Of the various causes of economic insecurity, unemployment is the most serious, partly because it is a risk which none can measure. It is possible to insure through an Insurance Company against loss of income through illness and old age and for death benefits, but not against the risk of losing one's job.

Now industrialisation has brought to mankind many advantages. It has made possible a standard of life far higher than could have been attained without it, but it has brought disadvantages as well, and the chief of these is unemployment. In primitive societies, such, for instance, as those found in the rural parts of China and India, almost every one is working on his own account on the land. Things may go well or ill with them, harvests may be good or bad, but there is always work for all. As a man grows old or infirm, the living he can win from his land may diminish, but so long as he can work at all, the work is there for him to do. But in an industrialised society, a man is either employed or unemployed. His income comes to him in the form of wage or salary, and the moment his employment ceases, this also ceases. Most workers are always exposed to the risk of losing their jobs through causes entirely beyond their control, and then, in spite of the National Unemployment Insurance Benefit, they may find themselves in serious financial difficulty if their unemployment is long continued.

No industrial system can be regarded as satisfactory which exposes the workers to so grave a risk. It is, of course, easy for industrialists to say that the responsibility for dealing with the problem of unemployment rests on the Government alone. Perhaps in future it may be found possible for the Government to afford greater security against hardship due to unemployment than it does to-day, but quite apart from the cost of doing this, experience has shown that the administrative problems involved would be serious, if, indeed, they were not found to be insuperable. At any rate, meanwhile the workers are suffering, and those who believe that it is possible, under our existing industrial system, to provide satisfactory conditions for the workers will certainly have to deal with this risk of hardship due to involuntary unemployment.

Recognising this fact, and pending any wider development of the State Scheme, in 1920 we inaugurated a scheme of unemployment benefit for our own work-people, applicable to every employee aged eighteen or over, no matter what his grade. Broadly, it provided for raising the unemployment benefits payable under the National Scheme to the following figures :—

(1) Fifty per cent. of the average earnings of the unemployed person ;

(2) Ten per cent. additional for a dependent wife ; and

(3) Five per cent. additional for each dependent child under sixteen years of age, or receiving full-time instruction at a school, university, college, or other educational establishment,

with a maximum of seventy-five per cent. of the average earnings, or £5 a week, whichever was the smaller, and a minimum of £1, 5s. a week (or £1 for those under twenty).

The amount of this provision and the period for which it is payable has been varied from time to time, but at the moment (June 1938) a fixed sum is paid of 8s. for a single person, 7s. additional for a dependent wife, and a further 2s. per week in respect of each dependent child up to a maximum of three children. These sums are paid for a period of one week for each four months of continuous employment since attaining the age of eighteen years. Thus, if an employee had been continuously employed for five years since his eighteenth birthday, he could draw the firm's benefit for fifteen weeks, if for ten years for thirty weeks, and so on.

The benefits derived from the firm's scheme, added to those derived from the National Scheme, bring the total benefits up to the following figures :—

| | Benefits derived from | | Total Benefits. |
	National Scheme.	Rowntree's Scheme.	
	s. d.	s. d.	s. d.
Men aged 21 but under 65 . .	17 0	8 0	25 0
Young men aged 18 but under 21	14 0	8 0	22 0
Boys aged 17 but under 18 . .	9 0	*	9 0
Boys under 17	6 0	*	6 0
Women aged 21 but under 65 .	15 0	8 0	23 0
Young women aged 18 but under 21	12 0	8 0	20 0
Girls aged 17 but under 18 . .	7 6	*	7 6
Girls under 17	5 0	*	5 0
Dependants' Benefits			
For an adult dependant . .	10 0	7 0	17 0
For a dependent child . .	3 0	2 0	5 0

* Not normally dismissed except for serious breach of discipline.

E

It is made a condition of receiving the company's unemployment benefit that the employee contributes not less than twopence either to his trade union unemployment insurance fund, or to any other fund whose regulations have been approved by the company. The benefits derived are in addition to those payable under our scheme.[1]

Partial unemployment benefit is payable in respect of any period which, owing to shortage of work through depression of trade, a worker suffers from short time. Such benefit is 2s a week for a single person, with a further 4s. for a dependent wife and 1s. additional for each dependent child up to a maximum of three children.

It may here be added that the general policy of the company is to deal, so far as reasonably possible, with any surplus of labour due to trade depression by working short time, rather than by dismissing a proportion of the workers. Such a policy is probably to the general advantage, so long as steps are taken to maintain the income of all at a level which will not cause serious hardship.

In order to finance the Unemployment Insurance Scheme, the company set aside, in the first instance, a lump sum of £10,000. It was originally thought that it would be necessary to put aside each year, commencing with 1921, sums equal to one per cent. of the wage bill until the Unemployment Fund reached £50,000 or five per cent. of the bill for the time being, whichever was the greater. Experience soon showed, however, that no such large reserve was needed, and at the present time only £5000 is

---

[1] This condition was imposed to meet the wishes of the trade unions, as they feared that our scheme, which provided benefits without any payment by the employee, might result in workers leaving the union, one of the inducements to remain in which was the fact that the union paid unemployment benefits.

maintained as a reserve, but the liability to pay one per cent. of the wage bill still remains.

Three of the features of the scheme (apart from the scale of benefits) which call for notice are, first, that the company does not guarantee the benefits, but only its fixed annual contribution ; second, that whilst the whole of the benefits are provided by the company, they are limited to those employees who independently insure themselves for additional unemployment insurance benefit by the payment of not less than 2d. per week ; and third, that the administration of the scheme is in the hands of an unemployment committee elected by the workers. It was felt that these conditions, and in particular the first and third, would constitute important safeguards against any attempt to take unfair advantage of the scheme. As a matter of fact, in practice we are not aware of any malingering or other improper conduct in regard to it. The total benefits paid under the scheme during the seventeen years in which it has been in operation are set out below :—

1921	.	£7,063	1929	. £10,473
1922	.	2,510	1930	. 13,785
1923	.	5,521	1931	. 9,033
1924	.	6,592	1932	. 4,806
1925	.	4,370	1933	. 2,025
1926	.	5,562	1934	. 1,132
1927	.	4,872	1935	. 449
1928	.	10,400	1936	. 304
1937	.	.	£947	

When it is remembered that the years in question included probably the worst years of trade depression ever faced by British industry, and when the scale of benefits is also taken into account, the surprising thing is the smallness of the cost in question. The scheme has done much to reduce anxiety on the part of the employees, and has been greatly appreciated. The Unemployment Scheme may be discontinued or amended by the company at any time, on giving three months' notice, and it is their intention to discontinue it if an adequate scheme of industrial or national insurance comes into force.

At the beginning of 1924, when we were making certain reductions in staff owing to improvements in organisation, we asked ourselves whether we could not do something more effective for the individuals affected than merely to increase their unemployment benefit. The view was stressed that what people needed was not so much a further increase in unemployment benefits as an alternative means of livelihood ; and the following steps were taken towards helping them to secure this :—

(1) In the first place, power was given to the unemployment committee to make lump sum payments to discharged employees in anticipation and in final settlement of the amounts of weekly benefit to which they might become entitled under the scheme. Thus, a man entitled to £2 a week for forty weeks might come along and say that whilst there was little prospect of his finding ordinary employment during the forty weeks, he did see his way to making a living, say, in a small business, if he could obtain a little capital. In such a case the unemployment committee were given power to settle his claim by paying a lump sum, say, £60 in place of the contingent liability to pay £2 per week for forty weeks. This power was supplemented by power to make loans.

The company set up a small Employment Advisory Committee consisting of a few members of the administrative staff, expert in different directions, to advise employees as to how they should go about finding alternative means of livelihood and to assist them in doing so. The method adopted was for the committee to search for possible openings and to advise employees on specific proposals submitted by them. Where a proposal, say, to commence a new business or to emigrate, was approved by the employee and the employment advisory committee, arrangements were made for the unemployment committee to make a lump sum in settlement of the claim to benefit. To this capital sum the employee was usually in a position to add the amount due to him from the pension fund. In this way capital was often made available in sufficient quantities, and this financial help was supplemented by expert advice on matters concerning the new venture. During the years 1928–32, 117 men were thus helped. Some took over shops or selling rounds, some set up boarding establishments or became inn-keepers, and some bought insurance agencies, while others turned to chimney sweeping, boot repairing, painting and decorating, poultry farming and market gardening, and three emigrated.

(2) Another step taken to help those we were obliged to discharge was to find whether other employers would engage any of them. An advertisement was inserted in many newspapers offering £2 a week for a year in respect of each individual taken on at a minimum of 55s. a week with a reasonable prospect of permanency. It was made a condition that no worker should be dismissed to find a place for one of our surplus men. As a result of this, a total of twenty-one men were placed, some going to London, others to Welwyn, and the remainder to a firm in York. The charges incurred under this arrangement were carried by the company's unemployment benefit scheme.

(3) Early in the year 1929, it became necessary to dispense with further men, and the directors decided to try to start new industries in York to which they

could be transferred. It was necessary to find industries which employed mainly adult male unskilled labour, and where good wages could ultimately be paid. As a result of much inquiry, three small industries were eventually started in York, accommodation being found for them in a building belonging to the company. Although each of the industries was under the direction of a man skilled in it, and although expert help was given both in financial control and selling methods, the experiment must, on the whole, be regarded as a failure. The men transferred found it extremely difficult to accustom themselves to work which was entirely different in character from their own, and where the wages were lower and the working conditions less agreeable than those to which they had been accustomed. Moreover, as it turned out, the experiment was made just at the beginning of the great trade depression of 1929–31. Even had the businesses been started without the handicap of being largely manned by workers without previous knowledge in them, it would have been extremely difficult, in the circumstances, to have established them successfully.

One of the industries is still being carried on. It lost considerable sums of money for a number of years, but is now paying. Another is still continuing, but has not been brought to the paying point, though it is now very close to it. The third business has been sold as a going concern, and is still continuing.

Unfortunately, the number of ex-Cocoa Works employees who are still after nine years engaged in any of the three businesses is very small.

(4) Another step which we took to find work for surplus workers was to induce a foreign manufacturer, who had decided to transfer his factory to England, to establish it in York. We did this by providing a portion of the necessary capital on terms which,

in the circumstances, would not have been provided by a bank or financial house. A condition of finding this help was that employment should be found for as many of our surplus men as possible. In this case again, it was found very difficult to fit many of our surplus men into a completely new industry, and although the business has been financially successful and has not involved our company in any loss, from the standpoint from which the experiment was undertaken, it must be written down as almost a failure.

(5) Another experiment which we made was to afford financial assistance to a company in York which was in need of further capital but was not in a position at the time to raise it through ordinary channels. The capital was provided on condition that a number of our surplus men should be employed. The result of this experiment has been very similar to that of the preceding one. It has not cost us anything in capital lost, but few of our surplus men could accustom themselves to work which was entirely unfamiliar to them.

Reviewing all the experiments that we made during those years when we had to dispense with a number of workers found to be surplus, it may be said that those made with a view to helping workers individually—whether by enabling them to set up a business on their own account or to emigrate, or in other ways, have, on the whole, met with a fair measure of success ; but the other experiments which we made to help our surplus workers have largely failed, and from the financial standpoint the failure has been a somewhat costly one to the company.

Of course, however, to help men after they have become unemployed is only second best. The best course is to prevent men from losing their jobs, and definite steps to that end have been taken at the Cocoa

Works. As will be shown later, it is not possible to dismiss a worker hastily or without sufficient cause. If a foreman or manager wishes to get rid of a man, he must explain the circumstances on a dismissal form, and send it to the employment manager for approval.   A worker is only dismissed as a last resort.   When a " round " man has been placed in a " square " hole, an attempt is made to rectify the error by transferring him to another job, and attempts are always made to regularise the demand for labour both as between one season of the year and another, and as between one department and another.   With care, a good deal can be done to reduce irregularity, and to increase the security of a man's work.   The task demands thought and detailed attention, but, from the human standpoint, it is well-directed effort.

Sickness

The directors hold the view that sickness, if not so long continued as to merge into chronic invalidity, is a risk against which it is possible for workers to insure, without financial help from the company other than that provided by the employer's contribution made under the National Health Insurance Act, 1911.   Under this Act as amended, practically all non-manual workers from the age of fourteen to seventy, whose earnings do not exceed £250 per annum, are compulsorily insured.   In the case of manual workers there is no wage limit.   The contributions are 10d. a week from employers for males and 7d. for females of sixteen years of age and upwards.   Workers pay similar amounts.[1]   The benefits are 15s. for males

---

[1] These weekly contributions, in addition to providing sickness benefits, provide old age pensions at sixty-five, and Widows' and Orphans' pensions under the Widows', Orphans' and Old Age Contributory Pensions Act, 1925.   (See p. 82.)

and 12s. for females for twenty-six weeks, after which they are reduced to 12s. and 7s. 6d. respectively.[1] Females receive 40s. maternity benefit. Juveniles under sixteen pay 2d. a week, employers paying a similar amount. They receive medical attention, but no money payment when sick.

The administration of the National Health Insurance is undertaken by existing Insurance Societies, most of which, having shown a surplus at the valuation, are now paying benefits in excess of those named above. Obviously, however, these amounts are inadequate for full maintenance during sickness, especially in the case of married men, who are normally responsible for the maintenance of dependants.

Most adult employees at the Cocoa Works are members of one or more sick clubs, so that they may receive adequate benefits when they are ill. Particulars of those connected with the Cocoa Works are given in Appendix II., p. 196 *et seq.*

Except in the case of salaried employees and over-lookers, the company makes no payment to workers who are absent through illness, but in cases of distress, help, varying with the individual needs of the employee, is given. These grants are to supplement National Health Insurance and sick club benefits, and to tide over the first week of return to work, when benefits cease and the wage earned has not been paid. The annual expenditure under this heading averages £600 a year. Members of the salaried staff receive full pay, less National Health Insurance, for the first six weeks of sickness in any year, and for the second six weeks they receive half-pay with no deduction. Any payments made after this depend on the circumstances of the case.

---

[1] Until 104 weeks have elapsed since entry into insurance, and 104 weekly contributions have been paid, the benefits are 9s. for men and 7s. 6d. for women.

CHRONIC INVALIDITY

Although it is possible for the workers, without undue sacrifice, to insure themselves against the risks of sickness of short duration, they cannot take similar precautions against illness which is long continued. After six months the sick benefits in many clubs are halved, and they usually cease entirely after twelve months. Thus, a family may be reduced to serious distress through the long-continued illness of the principal wage-earner, while in the case of his chronic invalidity there is usually no alternative to Public Assistance. From time to time, employees at the Cocoa Works have fallen victims to some lengthy illness, such as rheumatic fever, or have become chronic invalids. Such cases were considered on their merits, and more or less assistance was given, but no definite principles were followed in dealing with them, and the cost of each became a charge on the year's revenue.

In 1920 the directors felt that the time had come to create an Invalidity Insurance Fund, and to set up an organisation which would deal with all cases systematically. They did not think that invalidity was a risk against which they could expect all the workers to insure, for although cases of it are very distressing when they occur, they are, fortunately, so few and far between that the average worker would consider the danger too remote to be taken into account. The directors, therefore, decided to set apart a capital sum, the interest on which should be available for aiding cases of long-continued illness or chronic invalidity. Accordingly, in August 1920 they handed over to five trustees, 50,000 seven per cent. £1 Second Preference Shares in the company, providing a yearly income of £3,500. Of the trustees, who are all appointed by the directors, two are chosen from among the workers.

With certain exceptions, anyone who has been a member of the pension fund for not less than five years may, if off work through continued disability, apply for a grant. All grants are made by an executive committee of six persons, of whom three are appointed by the central council and three by the directors. In fixing the amount of a grant, and the instalments by which it is paid, the committee has regard to the amount of income, for the time being, in the hands of the trustees, and to the present and probable future demands thereon, and particularly to the needs of the applicant whose case is under consideration. The amount of assistance given varies with the applicant's financial position, with the number of dependants, and with other circumstances. It is laid down in the Trust Deed that :—

" except with the express sanction of the trustees, given in the particular case, no grant to any person shall during any one year from the date of the commencement of the grant, exceed the sum of £250, or such other sum as the trustees shall from time to time expressly sanction in lieu of the said sum of £250 as the yearly maximum amount of a grant."

As the fund was primarily created to deal with cases of chronic invalidity or long-continued illness, no grants are normally made to supplement benefits derivable from ordinary sick clubs during the first twenty-six weeks of invalidity. They are, however, made occasionally in special circumstances.

Since the fund was started in 1920, the total sum paid out in invalidity grants (including the help given to persons absent through short illness) has been about £59,000. The number of beneficiaries has been 335, of whom 28 suffering from chronic illness are receiving assistance from the fund at the present time (1938).

OLD AGE AND DEATH

Even after taking State Old Age Pensions into account, the vast majority of manual workers and lower paid executives cannot unaided lay aside enough during their working lives to enable them to look forward to old age without anxiety. It therefore becomes necessary for employers who desire to free them from such anxiety to inaugurate some scheme of old age pensions.   Many firms have instituted pension schemes for their employees. I propose in this section to indicate what we have done in this connection.

It must be admitted at once that any scheme involving such pensions as will actually relieve the workers of anxiety as to their old age, involves heavy cost, and many firms may hesitate to adopt it on that account.   But it is probable that those very firms may carry a heavy cost in " hidden pensions " on their weekly pay-rolls, without realising the fact. Let me make my meaning clear. If a firm establishes a liberal pension scheme, it will doubtless at the same time fix a definite retiring age, and will thus never find itself with a number of old workers of low working capacity drawing full pay.   In factories where there is no pension scheme it is common to find quite a number of old and feeble men and women. They are kept on because they have worked faithfully for a great number of years, and the management does not care to dismiss them.   Such employees are very costly ; not only does the firm lose on them individually but their presence tends to lower the pace, and lessen the output of the whole shop, especially where men are paid on a time and not on a piece basis. A liberal pension scheme is, therefore, not only an advantage to the workers, but to the employer, unless, of course, he is prepared to scrap his men ruthlessly as soon as advancing years render them inefficient. Employers of that type, fortunately, are becoming increasingly rare. But, if a retiring age is definitely fixed, the pensions then payable should, in fairness to the workers, be substantial in the case of those who join the service early in life. Men who join it after middle life cannot expect a large pension, but the retiring age must apply to them equally with the others. If they should consider it an injustice to be called on to retire on what they regard as an inadequate pension, they had better seek employment with a firm which has neither a pension scheme nor a fixed retiring age.

The object of the directors of the Cocoa Works in establishing a Pension Fund was twofold : first, as a matter of business, they recognised that it was desirable for men and women to retire at specified ages, and that this would involve considerable hardship unless a fairly liberal pension scheme was introduced. Second, they desired to remove from the minds of the workers anxiety with regard to their old age.

A pension scheme was established on 1st November 1906. Provision is made for retirement of male employees—both factory workers and the salaried staff—at the age of sixty-five, and of female employees at fifty-five, with optional retirement on adjusted pensions after sixty and fifty respectively. A slightly different scheme for retirement at sixty is in force for travellers and employees resident abroad. The earliest age at which members can enter the fund is twenty in the case of men and twenty-five in that of women.

The question may be asked whether, in practice,

these have proved to be the right retiring ages. I think there is no doubt that the answer is in the affirmative. Of course, there are those who not only would like to work longer, and could do so with advantage, but these are exceptions, and it is essential to the smooth working of the scheme that the retiring ages should apply universally. In fact, they apply also to directors, unless the board, for one year at a time, and for special reasons, invite a director to continue after sixty-five.

The pensions are derived from subscriptions paid by the employees, and contributions from the company. In all cases where membership ceases (on death or withdrawal) before pension age, the contributions of members are repayable, with $2\frac{1}{2}$ per cent. compound interest, either to the members or their legal personal representatives. Further, in the event of death after reaching pension age and before receipt of an amount of pension equal to the member's contributions plus $2\frac{1}{2}$ per cent. to date of pension age, the balance is payable to the late member's representatives. Thus, in no circumstances can any portion of a member's subscription revert to the fund. The subscriptions and pensions are on a fairly elastic scale, designed to meet varying circumstances, but the aim in view is that each member shall receive a pension of about fifty per cent. of the retiring salary or wage, and that the maximum subscription shall be five per cent. of the wage. This is secured in the great majority of cases, but a serious situation was created when, through the heavy reduction in the purchasing power of the £, leading to greatly increased wages, pensions, both actual and prospective, which bore a reasonable proportion to wages before the war, became quite inadequate under post-war conditions. To remedy this, it was necessary for the company to hand over a subvention of £73,000 to the fund, so as to raise to a higher figure the pensions of those who were too old to secure adequate pensions by increasing their contributions proportionately to the increase in their wages.

With the aid given by this subvention it has been possible to ensure that, except for a few men and women who joined late in life, no man will retire at sixty-five with a pension of less than 30s., and no woman at fifty-five with one of less than 20s. It must not be forgotten that, in addition to these pensions, workers will receive the State pension of 10s. payable to both men and women at sixty-five years.[1]

I need not give a table showing the exact sums payable by the employee to secure pensions of different amounts. These, of course, vary with the age on entering the scheme. But an idea of what these are may be gained by the following two examples, typical of a large proportion of the insured employees.

A man joining at twenty and paying 1s. a week till sixty-five would have a pension of 30s. a week, to which must be added the State pension of 10s. If he died leaving a widow, she would get from the company's Widows' Benefit Fund (see p. 81), subject to her being eligible for benefit, a minimum of 10s. weekly, together with 10s. from the State (see p. 82). If the man joined at thirty instead of twenty, his premium would be 1s. 6d. weekly instead of 1s. for the same benefit.

£500 a year is the highest pension for which an employee may subscribe.

---

[1] Women employees retire on pension at the age of fifty-five, but they do not become eligible for the State pension until they attain the age of sixty-five, and then only if they adopt one of two courses. They may either sign on regularly at the Employment Exchange as being available for work, or, alternatively, they may pay a premium of 1s. 6d. per week, and thus qualify for a pension of 10s. a week at sixty-five under the State Contributory Pension Scheme.

In practice, new male entrants generally subscribe for pensions of about £2 weekly at sixty-five, and pay an average premium of 2s. weekly, and women subscribe for £1 weekly at fifty-five, paying an average premium of 1s. 4d.

A special feature of our fund is that the company accepts the whole responsibility of guaranteeing its solvency. Should the experience be adverse, owing to light mortality, unwise investments, or other causes, the company and not the subscribers will have to bear the consequences. It is for this reason that it appoints four of the seven managing trustees, the remaining three being elected septennially by the subscribers. This representation of employees, namely, three out of seven—is quite sufficient to enable them to satisfy all subscribers as to the way in which the business of the fund is being conducted.

Membership of the pension fund is voluntary, but almost all eligible employees have joined it. With the authority of the members, the premiums are deducted from wages and salaries.

Cost of Pension Fund

We come now to the important question of the cost of the pension fund. As stated in a previous paragraph, the company has given an undertaking to keep the fund solvent. It guarantees a given pension for a given premium paid by the subscriber, and it must itself pay whatever premium the quinquennial valuations show to be necessary to secure that end. On 31st October 1936, the date of the most recent quinquennial valuation of the fund by its actuary, the fund had been in existence for thirty years and amounted to £1,165,234. During the thirty years, members' subscriptions, less refunds, have totalled about £340,000, while the company's total contributions during the same period were about £344,000. The balance of the fund is, of course, due to the cumulative effect of compound interest. The actuary found the fund amply solvent. The fund may now be regarded as having reached maturity, and the cost to the company can be forecast as not likely to exceed three and a half per cent. of the wages and salaries of the members, or two and a half per cent. of the total wages and salaries bill.

Widows' Pensions

As already stated, one object in founding the pension fund was to relieve the workers of anxiety as to their financial position in old age. So far as they themselves are concerned, the object was largely attained by the pension fund, but this did nothing to remove the fear of what might happen to a man's wife if she survived him, since his pension would cease on his death. To meet this situation, the directors, in 1917, inaugurated a Widows' Benefit Scheme, under which pensions are payable to all widows aged fifty and over at the death of the husband, subject, however, to the following limitations :—

(1) The parties must both have been under the age of fifty at the date of their marriage.

(2) The marriage must have preceded the death of the husband by at least ten years.

(3) The husband must have been, for an uninterrupted period of ten years prior to his death, a contributing member or pensioner of the fund.

The pensions are based upon the husband's pension or prospective pension at the time of his death, and range from thirty-five per cent. of that pension if the widow is fifty years of age, to fifty per cent. if

F

she is aged sixty-five or over. The minimum pension for a widow is 10s. weekly, and if the percentage of the husband's pension is less, it is made up to that amount.

This widows' pension scheme has been greatly appreciated, and men have stated that it has removed from their minds a grave anxiety. It has, however, proved a costly addition to the original pension fund, especially because so many men were advanced in years when the widows' scheme was introduced, and thus heavy new liabilities were incurred against which no previous payments had been made. Since 1st November 1917, £187,164 has been contributed by the company in respect of the widows' benefit fund. The present heavy cost will, however, not be permanent, being largely in the nature of back payment. Apart from this, it is estimated that a payment by the company equal to twenty-five per cent. of that made on behalf of the male members will suffice to provide the widows' benefit. In other words, the cost of the widows' pension scheme may be expected to amount to about one per cent. of the wage bill of male members of the pension fund or to about half per cent. of the company's total wages and salaries bill.[1] Unlike the main pension, the whole cost of the widows' pensions is borne by the company.

In addition to pensions payable to widows under the company's scheme, those who are eligible will receive substantial benefits under the Widows', Orphans' and Old Age Contributory Pensions Act of 1925, which covers all persons insured for the purpose of National Health Insurance, *i.e.* manual workers, and others whose salaries do not exceed £250.

---

[1] The difference between the two percentages is, of course, due to the facts that the one per cent. refers to the wages of men over twenty who are members of the pension fund, and the half per cent. to all wages paid by the company.

The benefits payable to widows under the national scheme are :—

10s. per week, plus
5s. per week for the eldest child, and
3s. for other children, if under fourteen years of age.

Death Benefit Scheme

In 1911 the suggestion was made to the directors, by the secretary of the pension fund, that for a comparatively small sum it would be possible to insure every married member for £50, made payable at such member's death.

The rules of the pension fund already provided that on the death of a member before pension age, the amount of his or her own subscriptions, with compound interest at $2\frac{1}{2}$ per cent., should be paid to his or her personal representatives. In order to provide a death benefit, the company undertook, in the case of a male member of the fund who died before entering into receipt of his pension, leaving a widow not herself entitled to a pension, or a child or children under fourteen, to provide a sum sufficient to bring the member's own subscription, with accumulated interest, up to £50. They also promised to make a similar provision in the case of any widow who was a member of the fund, and who died before entering into receipt of her pension, leaving a child or children under fourteen. The formation of the widows' fund in 1917 made provision for widows of older men ; the death benefit is only paid to those widows who do not receive pensions from the widows' benefit fund. In 1922 it was felt that the original benefit of £50 was inadequate, and the amount of the death benefit was increased to £100, or one year's prospective pension, whichever should be the greater. That this additional sum provided by the company may be utilised to the best advantage for the widow or children, the money is handed over to a committee consisting of the workers' trustees and the secretary of the pension fund, and two representatives of the labour department, who are held responsible for handling the money in such a manner as they may deem best.

It will be seen that under this scheme the liability of the company, heavy when a member first joins the fund, gradually disappears as his contributions increase. In the aggregate the cost to the company is slight when compared with the security given to the members. The total cost of the scheme for the twenty-five years 1912–1936 has been for seventy-three military cases £2,948, and eighty-nine civilian cases £4,386.

It was anticipated that the raising of the benefit in 1922 would increase the cost of the scheme to an average of about £400 per annum. Actually, during the fifteen years 1922–1936, the cost has totalled £3,253, an average of £217 per annum. The mortality among the younger men has been light ; mortality among the older men does not, as a rule, affect this scheme, but the Widows' Scheme. We consider this benefit a definitely valuable provision which has been made at a very low cost.

SUMMARY AND CONCLUSIONS

Let me briefly summarise the measures taken to afford to the workers a greater measure of economic security, and to consider how far they can be regarded as adequate. So far as unemployment is concerned, the company do what they can to avoid it, but with the best will in the world what they can do in this direction is strictly limited, especially as they are manufacturing goods which cannot, save to a limited degree, be made to stock. In the case of employees they are obliged to dismiss, they supplement by substantial amounts the benefits payable under the National Scheme. They have also adopted various measures to find work for those dismissed. But when all is said and done, it is clear that notwithstanding the immense improvement brought about by the National Unemployment Insurance Scheme, the problem of how to remove the menace of unemployment in our case and elsewhere remains unsolved. I say this, not forgetting what is done in this connection in other countries, for I am convinced that British workers would not tolerate the autocratic methods adopted in those countries which claim to have gone farthest in abolishing unemployment. No system of industry can, however, be regarded as satisfactory which leaves unsolved the problem of how to avoid hardship to individuals due to unemployment arising from causes beyond their control.

Turning now to the other causes of economic insecurity, the company does not normally make any voluntary contribution to sickness benefits, as they consider that, except in the case of sickness of long duration, the existing facilities for insurance are adequate, but the income on a capital sum set aside for the purpose, brings in £3,500 a year to provide assistance in cases of chronic illness.

As regards old age, the pension fund provides pensions for men at sixty-five and women at fifty-five which are only exceptionally less and usually more than half an employee's retiring wage. The cost of this scheme is divided between the company and the employees, the company paying rather over half. There is a pension scheme for pensioners' widows entirely paid for by the company, the pensions ranging from thirty-five per cent. to fifty per cent. of the husband's pension. All pensioners are insured for £100 at death.

When the special circumstances due to the sudden depreciation of money values have disappeared,[1] the total annual cost to the company of providing this will be about four per cent. of the total wages and salaries bill. This cost is in addition to the capital sums, amounting in all to £166,000, which have been contributed from time to time.

On the whole, I think the schemes afford a reasonably adequate measure of economic security for those who remain in the company's employment till they reach retiring age. But it must be pointed out that the security for old age depends on the continued association of the employee with the firm. Thus, if an employee were dismissed, or left the service to take up another appointment, he would be entitled to withdraw his own contributions to the pension fund, plus $2\frac{1}{2}$ per cent. compound interest, but he could lay no claim to the contribution made by the company year by year on his account. These would revert to the fund. Similarly, the claim to a widow's pension would be lost. To this extent the security is only partial.

It may be argued that, in view of the cost, it would be impossible, especially where labour constitutes a large proportion of the cost of production, for industry generally to provide security for the workers on a scale as liberal as I have described above. But as I have already said, many employers are now paying " hidden pensions," which I imagine are often much more costly than they ever realise. However, apart from this, I suggest that in one way or another, either with or without further state aid, a measure of security not less adequate than that described above is the least that should be regarded as satisfactory.

Improved conditions for the workers can only come

[1] These are described on p. 78.

from the margin between total production costs and net receipts. There is, therefore, a definite limit to what can be spent to improve their lot. Sooner or later they may have to decide whether they prefer to take all that share of the profits which industry can afford in the form of wages or salaries, etc., or a small part of it in the form of pensions. Meanwhile, our own experience suggests that a liberal pension scheme takes a heavy burden of anxiety from the shoulders of the workers, and is greatly appreciated by them.

CHAPTER IV

HOURS OF WORK

THE question of the length of the working week is much to the fore just now, and legislation limiting the hours of work has recently been passed in the U.S.A., France, and elsewhere. It is important that we should be clear regarding the considerations which should be borne in mind when deciding what the length of the working week should be. What emphasis, for instance, should be laid on the questions of health and upon the desirability of giving the workers more leisure, and how far is the argument sound that if hours of work are reduced employment will be found for more workers although the same weekly wage is to be paid for the shorter as for the longer week.

Dealing first with health, the number of hours the average worker can work without injury to health will depend on the character of the work, and on age and sex. An adult can work longer hours than a juvenile, and a man than a woman. Clearly none of these should work longer than they can do without overstrain. Since the exact number of hours which they can, from the health standpoint, suitably be asked to work will necessarily vary from industry to industry, no general figures can be given. I doubt whether a forty-eight hour week is excessive for men or women of normal strength, engaged on manual work of average severity, although it may be excessive for juveniles under eighteen. By saying that it is not excessive, I mean that I doubt whether health would be noticeably improved if the workers came to work on six days a week, but worked a total of,

AERIAL VIEW OF THE COCOA WORKS, showing :

1. Swimming Bath
2. The Theatre
3. Canteen and Class Rooms
4. Glass House, where cocoa, coffee, sugar cane,
   vanilla and many other of our raw materials
   are to be seen growing
5. Hard Tennis Courts
6. Some of the Playing Fields
7. The Rose Garden
8. Grass Tennis Courts
9. The Joseph Rowntree Library
10. Some of the Bicycle Sheds
11. One of the Motor Car Parks

The buildings cover 19 acres, and the superficial area
of all floors is over 36 acres. The total area of the
cocoa works estate is nearly 200 acres.

say, forty-four hours instead of forty-eight. On the
other hand, if the reduction of hours enables them to
work a five-day week, that would be of real benefit.

As regards the desirability of adding to the workers'
leisure, I think a strong case can be made out—but
here again the value of such action will be greatly
increased if the shortening of hours renders possible
a five-day week.

I do not think that the shortening of the working
week without lessening weekly wages will significantly
affect the number of persons employed. If the hourly
output per worker remains as before, then obviously
the cost of production must rise. This will tend to
put up selling prices and in turn to lower the workers'
real wages, so lessening the demand for goods, and therefore the volume of employment. But the workers'
hourly output may increase sufficiently to neutralise
the reduction of hours, through the workers working
faster, or wasting less time, e.g. starting more promptly
and working more nearly to leaving time ; or through
better organisation. In that case the number of
workers employed in the business will be the same
as before. Again, costs may be kept down to the
previous level by the use of labour-saving machinery,
and in that case the result would be that the number
of workers directly engaged in the manufacture of
a given volume of goods would be less than before,
but, on the other hand, a certain number of workers
would be required to make the " labour saving "
machines. In any case, there are no a priori reasons
to suppose that on balance the total number of people
employed would be any greater than before the hours
were reduced.

In view of the above considerations, I believe that
we may rightly rule out any beneficial effect on the
employment problem as a factor in favour of reducing
hours without reducing wages.

Up to 1895, at the Cocoa Works, we worked fifty-four hours a week in accordance with the usual practice at that time. Work for both men and women began at 6 a.m., and continued until 5 p.m. On Saturdays we worked from 6 a.m. to 1 p.m. In 1895, however, we reduced the hours to forty-eight per week, without altering day wages or piece rates, and we found that the earnings of piece-workers did not suffer in spite of this reduction. We have no record of its effect on the output of day workers, but the general impression left on my mind was that, taking the factory as a whole, there was no appreciable reduction of output. In April 1919 the hours were reduced to forty-four a week, as a result of negotiation with trade unions through the agency of the Interim Industrial Reconstruction Committee. Under the agreement with the unions, some of the largest firms in the industry, which were mentioned by name, agreed to reduce their hours to forty-four, other signatories to the agreement reducing their hours to forty-seven. We made no changes in weekly rates to day workers or in piece rates.

The central council at the Cocoa Works, consisting then of twenty-six workers elected by popular ballot, and twenty-six members of the administrative staff, were consulted as to what arrangement of working hours would suit the wishes of the employees. They suggested certain alternatives, and took a plebiscite of all the workers over eighteen years of age, to decide which course should be adopted. By a large majority it was decided to divide the week as follows :—

Monday and Friday : 7.30 a.m. to 5 p.m., with one hour for dinner.

Tuesday, Wednesday, and Thursday : 7.30 a.m. to 5.30 p.m., with one hour for dinner.

By this arrangement, employees were entirely free

from 5 p.m. on Friday until 7.30 on Monday morning.
It was thought by some, however, that many of the
girls, especially the younger ones, would not appreciate
the Saturday morning holiday, as they might be
expected to spend it in helping at home. Moreover,
it seemed possible that in the winter months employees
might prefer an arrangement of hours under which
they started later in the morning, instead of having
a whole holiday on Saturday. Accordingly, it was
agreed that the new arrangement should only be
binding for six months, after which the workers should
be consulted again. When, however, the question
of a possible change was mooted at the central works
council, at the end of six months, the workers' representatives stated emphatically that it would be a
waste of time to take a fresh plebiscite, as the universal
opinion was in favour of the existing arrangement
of hours. Undoubtedly, it is the long week-end which
is the most popular feature in the reduction of hours.
Had we continued to work on six days instead of
concentrating the forty-four hours' work on five days,
the reduction of hours would have been much less
appreciated.

The above arrangement applies to practically
every one in the factory working on the ordinary day
turns ; the exceptions being a few men in the packing
department and similar miscellaneous workers, a few
maintenance men and men on shifts and night work.
So far as possible these take their turns in working
on Saturdays, for which, of course, they receive extra
pay. The building staff does not keep the factory
hours. They have a forty-four hour week, but their
times of coming and going are regulated by the
National Building Council, and they work on
Saturdays.

A criticism sometimes urged against short hours,
and which is particularly pertinent in connection

with a division of working time which leaves Saturdays free, is that paid work may be undertaken by the workers in their " off " time. Our experience is that this only happens in an insignificant number of cases. Public opinion in the factory is strongly against such a procedure, as it is considered unfair for one man to do double work while others are unemployed.

The hours in the office are shorter than in the factory. Up to April 1919 they were forty-one and a half per week ; then they were reduced to thirty-nine and a half, and in December 1919 the hours were reduced to thirty-nine a week. The clerks prefer to come early, in order that they may leave early, and their working hours are from 8 a.m. to 12.30 p.m. and 2 p.m. to 5 p.m. on two days, and till 5.30 p.m. on the other three days of the week. The majority of them enjoy a free Saturday, only those attending who are required for essential work. Here, as in the factory, a few workers must be on duty for urgent work, but, so far as possible, they take turns in this, and work a shorter day on the earlier days of the week.

Rest Pauses

Both in the offices and the workrooms the girls have a recess of ten minutes in the morning, while in certain departments juveniles are allowed a break during the afternoon. In addition, girls working on certain machines in the offices are given two five-minute rest pauses at about 11.30 and 3.30. These breaks in production are not taken into account when calculating the time worked for wage-paying purposes. Facilities are provided for the purchase of light refreshments, and on the average of the year 1760 cups of tea, cocoa, or lemonade, 400 glasses of milk, and 600 cakes and pastries are sold daily. Some of the girl clerks go to the canteen, and others to departmental lunch rooms provided for this purpose, while some have refreshments taken to them in their own offices. In the factory, refreshments are served in the workrooms.

We have not accurately measured the effect of this break on output, but are of opinion that it is beneficial. Men and youths over eighteen have no similar break, but most boys under eighteen have a break for refreshments during the morning.

THE EFFECT OF SHORTENING HOURS ON TIME-KEEPING

One effect of the five-day week has been to improve time-keeping. Accurate statistics have been kept for some years to show the amount of time lost from all causes. The reasons given for lost time by employees are so often inaccurate that it is frequently not possible to analyse them, but all time lost, whether with or without leave, is registered, including holidays, except public holidays, when every one is off. In order, however, to distinguish between broken time for which a good reason (either holidays or *bona fide* illness) can definitely be assigned, and broken time which may or may not be satisfactorily accounted for, a distinction is drawn between those who are off for a whole week or more, and those who are off for less than a week. The following table shows the effect on time-keeping of the reduction of hours. The comparison is drawn between 1918 (the last year during which forty-eight hours were being worked) and the period December 1923–4, after the forty-four hour week had been introduced. Figures for 1936 are added to show how far the effect has been maintained (see p. 94).

In considering these figures considerable allowance must be made for the fact that the staff in 1918 included a large number of men graded C3. This, however, is not true of the women, and it will be noted that

	Average percentage of possible hours lost by employees.			Average percentage of possible hours lost by employees, *excluding those absent for a whole week.*		
	48 hours	44 hours 1923–4	1936 [1]	48 hours	44 hours 1923–4	1936
Factory—						
Men	7·3	3·4	3·5	2·7	1·2	1·5
Women	7·4	4·4	4·5	3·3	1·7	1·9

their time-keeping distinctly improved when the hours of work were reduced. Unfortunately, no pre-war figures are available, but there is no doubt that the five-day week led to a marked improvement in time-keeping.

Overtime and Short Time

Of course, the object of reducing the official working week will be largely defeated if the reduction in hours is purely nominal ; that is, if overtime is habitually worked. In a seasonal trade, such as that followed at the Cocoa Works, where there is a great rush before Christmas, it has not been found possible to eliminate overtime, but the amount of it is constantly watched. A return of the overtime and short time worked in every department is prepared monthly, and carefully examined with a view to seeing whether work can be regularised. Children under sixteen are only permitted to work overtime in very exceptional circumstances, and for short periods. Even then the arrangement must have the express sanction of a director. Where there is the likelihood of overtime in one department

[1] I give the figures for 1936 rather than those for 1937, because the figures for the latter year were abnormally high. This was partly due to a severe epidemic of influenza, lasting for two months, and partly to the fact that we were, for some months, working overtime to an extent which was quite exceptional. The average percentage of hours off in 1937 was :—men 4·2 per cent., women 5·7 per cent., or, excluding those off for a whole week, 1·9 per cent. and 2·5 per cent.

and short time in another, attempts are made to transfer workers. It is also sought to meet seasonal pressure by manufacturing goods in the slack season which will be required in the busy season, but this can only be done to a limited extent in an industry such as ours where goods must be sent out fresh. Short time in the chocolate departments occasionally occurs in hot weather, when the heat renders the manipulation of the chocolate impossible. In accordance with the Industrial Agreement which governs many of the working conditions at the Cocoa Works, short time due to weather conditions is paid for at the rate of about two-thirds of the minimum day wage. The total time lost through this cause is not great, as many of the rooms are air-conditioned.

SHIFT WORK

Of the males working at the Cocoa Works at the end of 1937, exclusive of the building, engineering, and office staffs, fifty-four per cent. worked ordinary day shifts, eighteen per cent. were on night work, and twenty-eight per cent. worked on the two or three shift system. All workers work forty-four hours a week, the hours of the shift workers in most cases being 6 a.m. to 2 p.m., 2 p.m. to 10 p.m., and 10 p.m. to 6 a.m.

It is recognised by the directors that from the social standpoint, night work and shift work are undesirable, but the buildings and machinery involved are so costly as to make it almost impossible for one firm acting alone to work on a one-shift basis. Moreover, part of the work, by its nature, involves continuous production throughout the twenty-four hours.

THE EFFECT ON OUTPUT OF SHORTENING HOURS

We have found it extremely difficult to measure the precise effect on output of the shortening of hours to forty-four a week, because in 1919, when the change occurred, the factory was reverting from war to peace conditions. 1700 men who had been serving with the colours were returning to work ; the character of the goods manufactured was changing, and many other adaptations were taking place. Still, although no accurate measurement was possible, such figures as we were able to collect confirmed the general opinion of those best acquainted with the facts, that in the case of pure handwork scarcely any reduction in output was experienced as the result of the shorter hours ; while in some of the machine departments there was a certain reduction which was never large, but varied according to circumstances. Taking the factory as a whole, and reviewing the matter after nineteen years' experience, I am inclined to think that, taking everything into account, the cost of production has not been significantly increased by the reduction in working hours. In those cases where the immediate effect of the shortening of hours was to increase the cost of production, that fact has led to a quickening of the effort to bring about improvements in production methods in other directions to neutralise this. On the whole, therefore, I think it may be said that the reduction in hours has been fully justified, and, undoubtedly, the workers immensely appreciate the free Saturday.

Could Hours with Advantage be Further Reduced ?

The question naturally arises whether forty-four hours is the minimum week which can be advantageously worked. I have discussed the matter with the doctors and members of the staff of the labour department who are particularly concerned with the health of the workers, and am satisfied that no further reduction of hours is called for on grounds of health. In the case of young workers, a little over-time occasionally is not found to be prejudicial to health, but if overtime were regularly worked, it would be harmful. In connection with this matter, it must be remembered that although I am speaking of a forty-four hour week, young workers do not actually work this number of hours. The boys are away from the factory at classes for a whole morning or afternoon each week, and the girls for two separate hours; and, in addition, they have rest pauses that aggregate fifty minutes in the week. A further point to be noted is that the workers are all examined by the doctor before engagement, and allocated to jobs suited to their physical strength.

Of course, if the same output could be obtained in less time without undue strain, a yet shorter week might be advisable. But any reduction of hours which involved a lessening of output, and, conse-quently, inability to pay adequate wages, would be against the interests of the workers.

HOLIDAYS

By a provision of the Industrial Agreement already referred to, workers are entitled to payment for six public holidays and a week's summer holiday in the year. According to the terms of the Agreement, the payment in the case of piece-workers is not to be their average earnings, but the minimum rate of pay for workers of their age.[1] The week's holiday was first introduced at the Cocoa Works in 1919. Public holidays had, since 1910, been paid to all members

[1] In our case, while approving the agreement regarding holiday payment, we have, early each year, considered whether we could afford to pay piece-workers for holidays on the basis of average earnings, and have done so whenever the prospects for the year's trading were favourable.

G

of the Pension Fund, *i.e.* to practically all regular male employees of twenty years of age and upwards, and all female employees of twenty-five years of age and over. The payment for public holidays became universal in 1919. Members of the clerical staff have a fortnight's holiday in addition to the statutory public holidays. The following scale of fixed holiday allowances for all higher grades has recently been put into force :—

1.   *Overlookers*—
Grade " A " . . . . 2½ weeks
Grade " B " . . . . 2 ,,
Certain minor supervisory grades 1½ ,,

2. *Travelling Staff*—
Divisional Sales Managers . . 4 ,,
District Sales Superintendents . 3 ,,
Travellers . . . . 2 ,,

3. *All other staffs*—
Holiday allowances vary from two to four weeks, in some cases according to salary, and in others according to grade.

All these holidays are in addition to the six public holidays.

The length of holiday does not vary with length of service. It is felt that the right basis for variation is the value of the service rendered, or the strain which it involves, and not the number of years for which it is continued.

CHAPTER V

THE LABOUR DEPARTMENT

ALTHOUGH it is important to surround workers with good material conditions, it is even more important to create and maintain what perhaps I can best describe as a "personal environment" which will encourage each individual to be and to do his best. The ideal at which we should aim is that every one should work with as much enjoyment, energy, and intelligence as if he were working on his own account. This, of course, is a very high ideal, which probably has never been realised, though I have occasionally visited factories which very nearly attained it. In seeking to create such a spirit, the first thing is for those in positions of responsibility to recognise that the workers are something more than profit-producing instruments. They are not simply a means to an ulterior end. On the contrary, their personal welfare is an important end in itself, though not the only one for which the factory exists. Much, probably most, of the unrest from which industry has suffered for so long, and is suffering so acutely at present, is due to the failure on the part of employers to recognise this fact. Largely through lack of clear and independent thinking, we have been inclined to look upon those working in our factories in the mass, and to speak of them as "hands." We have not had imagination enough mentally to separate the mass into its constituent units. We have failed to realise that five hundred "hands" are really five hundred individuals, each with a personality as sensitive to its environment as yours or mine.

Now it is just as fatal an error to treat workers in the mass as it would be to treat machinery in the mass—a thing no one would dream of doing. Quite apart from the human aspect of the question, and for the moment considering the workers solely as instruments of production, such an impersonal way of regarding them is a serious flaw in our method of business administration. Every worker should be looked upon as an individual and encouraged to contribute his individual quota to the success of the firm. This is the policy we naturally adopt when we work with two or three persons, but can it be carried out in a large factory where hundreds or thousands are employed ? Yes, it can, but only as the result of a considered policy supported by an adequate organisation. The managing director, or works manager in a large factory, cannot give the necessary detailed attention to this side of the business any more than he can personally attend to each machine, and so, if it is not to be neglected, adequate steps must be taken to look after the labour force, just as they are taken to look after the function of production or sales.

In our factory all labour matters, and by that I mean almost all the matters discussed in this book, are under the control of one of the directors. He is responsible for seeing that the " human factor in business " is not neglected and that a progressive labour policy is adopted. On him devolves the responsibility for thinking out and developing the company's labour policies, and after he has secured the approval of the board, it is for him to see that they are carried out.

But although the post of labour director is by no means a sinecure, he has other duties to perform, and it necessarily follows that the day-to-day management of the department must be undertaken by its manager.

The labour manager should be a man having true sympathy with the workers, but he must not be a sentimentalist. He must see the point of view of the management as well as that of the workers, for if he is to succeed in his work, he must win the confidence not only of the workers but also of the management. Indeed, these qualities are required by all those in the labour department who have to deal with the workers. Having regard to the importance which the directors attach to labour matters, it follows that the labour manager's position is one of real authority. He ranks as one of the half-dozen or so functional managers outside of the York Board.

He is responsible for all wage and labour questions in the works, and for all educational and recreational activities. By reason of his expert knowledge, he is the responsible officer associated with the labour director in all specially important negotiations with trade unions, and he himself deals with the unions on ordinary matters. His two chief assistants are the men's and women's employment officers, who are responsible among other things for the engagement and dismissal of all labour, and its transference, when necessary, from one department to another. In addition, he controls the wages section, all recreational and educational activities, the medical and psychological departments, and the canteen.

I propose in this chapter to describe such parts of the work of the labour department as may be of interest to others, and which are not described elsewhere in this book.

Engaging New Employees

All male labour is engaged through the men's employment department, except clerks and salaried staff, who are engaged through the clerical staff office. Originally, every foreman or departmental manager engaged his own workers, but this custom was discarded many years ago. It is the duty of the employment manager to maintain a list of all applicants for employment, and to keep in touch with all likely sources of supply. Engagements are usually made from this list, or, failing this, from the local Employment Exchange, with which the closest contact is maintained. The applicant who appears to be the most suitable is submitted to the doctor, and, in the case of young persons under twenty-one, to the psychological department for examination. If their reports are favourable, the employment manager effects the engagement. In the case of skilled tradesmen, the chief engineer or the architect sends a representative to test the applicant's technical ability, but the actual engagement is made by the employment manager. It is his responsibility to notify the time-keeper and wage office when persons are engaged, and to maintain records of all employees.

Promotions

Vacancies offering an opportunity of promotion arising within a department are, in accordance with the general rule of the company, advertised within that department. The departmental manager deals with all such appointments himself, generally consulting the psychological department on the question of the suitability of the applicant he prefers, and the employment department when he has decided which candidate he proposes to appoint to the job. Should he be unable to find the right type of man in his own department, he informs the employment manager, who then advertises the vacancy throughout the works, stating the nature of the job, the qualifications required, and the salary offered. In these circumstances, the appointment is made by the employment manager in consultation with the departmental manager, the former negotiating any departmental transfer that may be necessary.

The labour director keeps a list of all persons who have shown evidence that they possess qualifications which may in time fit them to fill administrative posts. Such workers are carefully watched, and opportunities given them to develop their powers. Periodically, the labour director goes through the list and inquires in the different departments whether any new names should be added to it. When an administrative vacancy arises, this list is examined to make sure that any possible candidate is not overlooked, even although he may not have applied for an advertised post. Similarly, it is part of the employment manager's duty to keep his eyes open for employees who appear to have special qualifications, so that he may be in a position to make recommendations to managers who want men qualified for different kinds of work. In making a list of such men, he is greatly helped by the findings of the psychological examinations.

The engagement of employees, especially when they are young, should never be a slipshod or hurried performance. The interview on engagement is a valuable means of giving the new worker, at the very beginning, the right kind of outlook. It makes a great difference whether a man or boy is hurriedly " put on " by a foreman who is principally concerned with production, or engaged by a man chosen for his sympathetic insight into character, and connected solely with the personal side of business administration. The interview should take place in private, in a suitably furnished office ; and if the applicants have to wait, they should do so in a comfortable room. The applicant should be told something of the

spirit in which it is sought to conduct the factory—
a spirit of mutual goodwill, in which both the management and the workers give of their best. It is not
a matter of simply " setting on an extra hand," but
of seeking the co-operation of another colleague.
To convey the idea that we are bestowing a favour
when we are employing a man is to introduce the
wrong spirit from the start. We are, on the contrary,
making a contract which it is expected will be mutually
advantageous.

In addition to engaging new employees, the employment manager is responsible for all departmental
transfers. Any departmental manager whose work
is growing slack advises the employment section that
he will soon have to dispense, either temporarily or
permanently, with a certain number of workers.
The employment manager then seeks to place them
elsewhere in the factory. Managers are urged to give
as long notice as possible of a prospective surplus of
workers so as to avoid dismissals.

DISMISSING EMPLOYEES

Should an overlooker wish to dismiss a man for
any reason other than shortage of work, he first
sees the departmental manager, who, if he agrees,
fills in a form stating why the dismissal is recommended.
This is referred to the employment manager, who
investigates it in consultation with the chief shop
steward. If dismissal is decided on, it is carried
out by the employment manager. The above procedure not only ensures co-ordination throughout the
works in this matter, but obviates the risk of dismissal
for inadequate reasons. Sometimes, for instance, a
man's failure to make good in one department may
be due not to any intrinsic fault, but to the fact that

he is a "square peg in a round hole," a situation which can be remedied by transfer to another department.

Whenever employees are to be dismissed owing to shortage of work, their names are submitted by the departmental manager to the shop steward, who, as stated on p. 34, has full opportunity to criticise the list of those selected for dismissal. A detailed record of each employee is kept and is available for reference should an application for re-engagement be received.

Foremen and departmental managers elsewhere, who have the power of dismissal in their own hands, may imagine that the arrangement outlined above would seriously undermine their authority. Save in the case of that rapidly disappearing class of foremen who can only rule by fear, this is not the case. If a foreman has good reason for demanding a man's dismissal, he will always be able to carry his point, and in the absence of such good reason he has no right to ask for his dismissal.

Investigating Complaints

Another important function of the employment manager is the investigation of complaints. No matter how well managed a factory may be, there will always arise a number of personal grievances, which should be carefully examined. "Rough justice" is not enough. Every personal grievance should be promptly investigated, and explained away if imaginary, or removed if real. Without in any way encouraging mere fault-finding or tale-bearing, it is important to provide means for the easy ventilation of a sense of injury. The labour manager and the members of his staff, especially the employment manager and the chief shop steward, are always ready to listen to anyone who has, or thinks he has, a grievance.

But it is not only complaints which the workers bring to the labour manager and his staff. Sometimes they want to discuss personal difficulties, and are glad of the help which can often be given them to find a " way out."

Women's Section of the Labour Department

The organisation of the women's employment department is very similar to that of the men. But most of the girls come to us straight from school, and consequently they apply for work in batches at the end of the school terms. This enables us to give more careful attention to their initiation to the works than is possible in the case of boys who come at irregular intervals. Moreover, girls are more sensitive than boys, and it is therefore more important to give them the right start.

We used to have what we called a preparatory school, which all new girls attended as soon as they were engaged. It lasted for five days, and the girls were paid wages while attending. In that school the girls were addressed by different people on a number of subjects connected with the factory, and these talks were interspersed by games, visits to different parts of the factory, and talks illustrated by lantern slides showing how the raw materials we use, such as cocoa, sugar, gum arabic, etc., are grown and transported to York. But experience has taught us that while the school was undoubtedly of value, it was on much too complicated a scale. We were trying to teach youngsters too much in too short a time. To-day, therefore, our methods are quite different. We seek to teach them what we did before, but to do it gradually.

The formal school only lasts for half a day, which is spent as follows :—

On the day she starts, a girl's mother is invited to come and see her daughter at work, and is introduced to her personnel assistant and forewoman.

Below—

Carefully selected senior workers teach the new entrant by methods prescribed by the motion study section, under the supervision of one of the Works' psychologists.

9.0 a.m.   Met by member of labour department ; taken to time office for numbers, fitted up with overalls, briefly examined by dentist.

9.20 a.m.   Introductory talk by member of labour department.

9.30 a.m.   Talk on wages by the labour manager.

10.0 a.m.   Talk on more important workroom rules (those bearing on foreign substances, theft, time-keeping) by a personnel assistant.

10.20 a.m.   Break.

10.30 a.m.   Tour of the works.

12.30 p.m.   Those staying to dinner are introduced to the canteen assistant, who explains the canteen check system, and sees that they have a table at which to sit.

1.30 p.m.   Met by their forewoman at the time office, and shown by her how to clock, and clocking rules explained. Then they are taken to the cloakroom, where the importance of marking overalls, and rules with regard to washing, leaving overalls at the factory during the week, etc., are explained. After this they are taken to the workroom, and shown where to put their lunches and dinners.

The forewoman introduces the new girls to their charge-hands and trainers, and occasionally to fellow-workers. She stresses the fact that the girls are not to be afraid to ask questions, and that the personnel assistant will always be glad to help them in any difficulty.

For the first week new girls start work at 9 a.m.

The filling in of wage forms is taught gradually, the teachers entering output until the girls learn how to keep their own records.

In the afternoon of the day on which a girl begins work, her mother is invited to tea, where she meets the girl's forewoman and personnel assistant, and is then shown into the workroom to see her girl at work. This bond between home and factory is much appreciated.

The information which used to be given in concentrated form in the five-day school is now given gradually in various ways. For instance, the talk about the raw materials we use is given them in the day continuation school, and the teachers there also see that the girls get to know all about the clubs, evening classes, camps, and so forth connected with the works. Much is also done by the trainers who are teaching the children the particular processes on which they are to be engaged ; they are urged to enter into sympathetic and understanding relationship with their pupils.

In addition to the miscellaneous information given in the way described above, each new employee is handed a leaflet containing information about the works, which it is necessary for them to have.[1]

The programme followed in the case of girl clerks joining the service is different. The following one is typical of the usual practice :—

9.0 a.m.	Talk—The Offices : What they Do and Why, by the office manager.
9.45 a.m. to 10.15 a.m.	Talk—The House of Rowntree, by the director in charge of the offices.
10.15 a.m. to 10.30 a.m.	Break.
10.30 a.m. to 11.15 a.m.	Talk—Works Councils, Associated Companies, Recreational Facilities, Educational Facilities, by a member of labour department staff.
2.30 p.m.	Works tour.

I have stated why it is more important in the case of girls than in that of boys that they should be given just the right start when they come to work ; but that is not enough. Our experience is that at all times, speaking generally, female employees require more careful supervision than men. This is partly because many of them are physically weaker, and partly because their age, on the average, is much lower than that of the men, and they are less able to look after their own interests. Again, they are more sen-

---

[1] A copy of this leaflet is given in the Appendix, p. 229 *et seq.*

sitive and emotional, and hence it is imperative to avoid friction, and to dispel even the shadow of a grievance. Consequently, at the time when the first edition of this book was written in 1921, we had, attached to each department where any considerable number of girls were employed, an officer called a "Girls' Supervisor." She was held responsible for the welfare of the girls in her department, but was not in any way directly concerned with its actual work. Experience, however, has shown that the more closely welfare activities are woven into the ordinary conduct of the business, instead of being something apart, the better it is both for the welfare of the girls and the success of the business. Consequently, the "girls' supervisors," while continuing to safeguard the welfare of the girls, have now been given other duties, acting as assistants to the managers of the departments on all matters connected with personnel. They were all chosen on account of their interest in the welfare of the girls, and still regard the furthering of this as an essential part of their work. These officers are now called "personnel assistants," and they have been transferred from the staff of the labour department to the staffs of the different departmental managers. They remain responsible to the labour department for the methods they employ, and their appointment and promotion are on the initiative of that department, always with the agreement of the appropriate departmental manager. Below is given a list of their duties :—

1. *Engagements.*

The personnel assistant has a talk with new girls allocated to her department on the day they start work. She also has an opportunity of meeting those parents who take advantage of the firm's invitation to visit the factory and take tea with the overlookers and personnel assistants, and to see their daughters at work on their first day.

2. *Training*.

In co-operation with the psychological department the personnel assistant ensures that each worker receives proper training in the work for which she is selected, and that any difficulties which would tend to interfere with the progress of training are as far as possible avoided.

3. *Transfers*.

When notified that work requires the transfer of girls from one section or department to another, the personnel assistant is responsible for seeing that suitable girls are selected. She also notifies the shop steward and the girls who are to be transferred of the terms of wage payment, after consultation with the proper authority.

4. *Wages*.

Although the personnel assistant has no power to fix wages, she is responsible for seeing that each girl in her department earns the wage fixed as the standard for her age. When a girl's earnings are unduly low, she must find out the reasons for this, and try to remove them. Sometimes the girl is finding difficulties with her work which she can help her to overcome. But sometimes other action is called for ; for instance, the work may be unsuitable, and after consultation with the psychological department, the girl is transferred. If a girl does not improve after every encouragement, together with training and careful supervision, the only course open to the personnel assistant is to report to the employment department that the girl appears to be unsuitable for any work available in the factory, and to recommend her dismissal.

5. *Time-keeping*.

The personnel assistant deals with all reports concerning bad time-keeping and with requests for leave of absence ; and in respect of both these matters, takes what action she considers necessary.

6. *General Conditions*.

The personnel assistant is responsible for watching the general welfare conditions of the rooms, such as ventilation, cleanliness both of the workrooms and of cloakrooms and lavatories, sufficiency of cloakroom and lavatory accommodation, and general workroom amenities. It is her duty to draw the attention of the responsible administrative officer to any conditions which she regards as unsatisfactory.

7. *Discipline*.

The personnel assistant is the manager's representative in matters of discipline, and forewomen report any breaches of discipline to her for treatment.

8. *Visiting*.

As the medical department is responsible for sick visiting, the personnel assistant visits only in exceptional cases.

9. *Savings Fund*.

Personnel assistants are responsible for the girls' savings fund collection.

10. *Medical*.

The personnel assistant is responsible for notifying the medical department of any alterations in working conditions or any new jobs which in her opinion should be inspected by a doctor. In the case of girls passed by the doctor as suitable only for certain types of work, she is required to see that girls are not put on to jobs for which they are not medically passed. The departmental rest room is under her control, and all accidents are reported to her.

11. *Relations with the Trade Union.*

The personnel assistant takes up any complaints or requests which the workers wish to put before the management. She is expected to obtain the co-operation of the shop stewards, and to explain to them the reason for managerial action in any specific case.

12. *Accessibility of Personnel Assistants.*

Any girl in the department may, at any time, go to see the personnel assistant, having first asked permission of the overlooker. She need not give any reason for wishing to see her.

13. *Social and Recreational.*

The directors rely upon the personnel assistants to do all in their power to encourage the girls to take advantage of the recreational and educational opportunities provided by the firm.

In two departments where large numbers of boys and youths are employed, male personnel assistants have recently been appointed, whose duties are parallel to those of the women personnel assistants.

Vocational Selection

No account of the steps taken in the Cocoa Works in connection with the engagement and dismissal of employees would be complete without a description of the work of the psychological department.

In 1921 a few of us came to the conclusion that a trained psychologist could help in selecting employees for different kinds of work, but to adopt such a course would have caused endless suspicion among the workers unless the whole thing was explained to them in the greatest detail. It was therefore necessary, before proceeding to the appointment of a psychologist, to discuss the proposition at great length in the central council. Psychologists were asked to come and lecture at the Cocoa Works, explaining exactly how psychology could help in the selection of workers. At first there was strong opposition to our proposal, but gradually, as the workers came to understand just what was involved, the opposition died down, and at the beginning of 1922 our first psychologist was appointed, and he began the investigation of the types of employees who were engaged in various occupations in the factory. He attempted to arrange a series of vocational tests which would increase the probability of accurate selection of new workers. Although the psychologist was fully informed of the latest work on vocational selection from the academic point of view, it was some months before he was able to get satisfactory results in the factory. It was quickly found that the academic type of psychological test in its original form was not suited to factory conditions, so tests were devised which, while embodying the essential principles of academic tests, were presented in a form more closely resembling factory conditions. It was found that tests involving the use of pencil and paper did not give satisfactory results for workers who were engaged on purely manual work, and some sort of performance test had to be substituted. Tests arranged for the selection of clerical workers were not affected in this way.

H

Having determined the type of test which was likely to give the most satisfactory results for the factory workers, the first year of work was taken up in determining exactly what tests were suitable for each type of job, and standards of performance on each test were determined by comparing the opinions of overlookers with the score obtained upon individual tests.

Psychological tests were devised at first only for one or two main types of work ; but with increasing success in the selection of workers engaged in these particular occupations, requests for assistance in the selection of other types of workers were received. The time occupied in testing an individual at the end of the first year's work was, however, so great as to be entirely unsatisfactory from the point of view of practical application in the factory, and so the early tests were reconsidered. The policy of having a definite series of tests for each type of occupation had been adopted in accordance with the common practice in academical work. As there are so many different jobs in a large factory, it became evident that it would be impossible to have a series of distinct tests for each type of work, if each worker, whose capabilities were entirely unknown, had to be examined for each type of occupation. After careful investigation a single series of tests was evolved, by the use of which it is now possible to determine which of the whole range of occupations in the factory is likely to suit a new worker. This series or " battery " of tests occupies about twenty minutes if applied to a single individual, or an hour if applied to a group of half a dozen workers at the same time, and is found to be of practical use under all conditions.

Psychological tests are applied in all cases where girls are employed, but have not been applied so extensively to men. The reason for this is not because the tests are not so successful in their case, but because a large majority of the jobs for which men are wanted are either those in skilled trades such as joiners, engineers, and so on, for which fully apprenticed workers are engaged, or constitute general labouring work for which no particular aptitude is required ; so that vocational selection, though helpful, would not give the workers or the firm such a noticeable advantage. Since 1935 certain of the " performance " tests have been applied to male applicants for work up to twenty-one years of age, and to adult men who seek promotion. Apprentices for skilled trades are selected by a written intelligence test and a short practical test, at which the prospective overlooker is present. Written tests are employed when selecting youths for clerical vacancies.

After nearly sixteen years' experience of vocational selection, I am in a position to say that it has completely justified itself. It has reduced the number of misfits and the time taken to train selected workers. Whereas in the case of girls under the previous system of selection, we had, within the first eighteen months of their training, to dismiss about twenty per cent. of those engaged, the proportion to-day is only about five per cent.[1] Moreover, the learning period in the case of beginners has been noticeably reduced in length, and the number who failed to reach proficiency in the standard time has been reduced to almost nil. Again, the number of those workers who have to be transferred from work to which they were originally put to another occupation, for reasons of inefficiency, has also been materially reduced. While the reduction of this waste of human effort has been of considerable

[1] The proportion of misfits during some recent years has exceeded five per cent., but only because, owing to labour shortage, it was temporarily necessary to engage a number of girls against the advice of the psychologist.

financial advantage to the employer, it has also resulted in a noticeable benefit to the workers. Learners who reach efficiency in a shorter time consequently reach their higher wage rates more rapidly than previously. One important result of vocational selection is that it undoubtedly reduces the proportion of workers who find their work monotonous. Workers who are engaged on occupations for which psychological tests show them to be ideally qualified have not, to our knowledge, complained of monotony, and would probably be unwilling to change their jobs for others which are popularly considered to be more interesting, thus indicating that monotony is relative to a particular worker, and not to a particular job.

When investigating cases of workers whose earnings were low, or who were inattentive and did bad work, it has almost always been found that there was something lacking in their psychological make-up. Without going too much into technical details, it may be interesting to note that one of the chief factors which determines whether or not a worker will be successful on a particular job is the degree of power of consecutive concentration or attention which he is able, easily, to bring to bear on the day's work. To adapt himself satisfactorily to work which is commonly considered to be monotonous, a worker should be one who does not easily concentrate for long periods on one subject, and whose attention can easily be diverted. If he has more than this abnormally low degree of concentration and attention he will find the work irksome, as there is not enough in the work itself to hold his attention and a sense of boredom results. Conversely, work which is popularly considered to be interesting will, to the worker of the first type mentioned, be not only difficult, but probably impossible. It may be interesting to note that in cases where the selection of workers is ideal we have noted a reduction in the number of accidents.

One is sometimes asked whether, if intelligence tests were generally employed in industry, the sub-average proportion of the population would be left without any opportunity of employment. Our experience goes to show that it is just as much a mistake to put a worker of high intelligence on a job demanding low intelligence as *vice versa*. We find that certain of our jobs call for workers of low intelligence, and that, indeed, in our case at least, the proportion of such jobs appears to be substantially equal to the proportion of sub-average applicants. Whether this will be found to be so throughout all industry, I cannot say. Whereas, therefore, formerly our women's employment officer often rejected girls on the ground that they had only reached fourth or fifth standard at school, now in certain cases she engages those who had not even reached these standards, being satisfied that they will make good on the jobs for which they are selected.

I think it may be said that, if anything, vocational selection tests are even more valuable in the case of office workers than in that of manual workers. Some kinds of office work are very routine in character, while others require constant thought and considerable concentration. By psychological tests it is possible, with considerable accuracy, to judge for which kind of work a particular applicant is best suited. This leads to a higher degree both of contentment and efficiency in the office.

When vocational tests were first introduced they were regarded with a good deal of suspicion, and in some quarters were resisted for a short time, but by handling the situation carefully, and maintaining the closest co-operation between the psychologist and the official representatives of the workers, the suspicion soon died down, and the workers came to realise that they had nothing to fear from the innovation. A few instances of inefficient workers who had been given their notices were taken up by the psychological department at the request of the workers' representatives. After psychological tests, some of these, instead of being dismissed, were transferred to other jobs, in which, because the work was suitable for men of their temperaments, they made good. Cases like this rapidly became known. To-day, vocational selection is looked on throughout the works as a normal item in the factory routine. It is generally recognised that by helping to fit individuals into the jobs for which they are permanently suited, vocational selection has given them a larger degree of happiness and satisfaction in their work than would formerly have been possible.[1]

Training of Workers

A word may be added here with regard to the methods we adopt for the training of our junior workers, especially girls. A good system of training is a logical complement to a good system of selection. Although the women actually engaged in training are on the staffs of the production managers, they are supervised by members of the psychological department, who are also responsible for working out the method of training. The trainers, who give their whole time to the work, are selected from among the workers, selection depending principally upon personality and temperament. The quality of their work as piece-workers should be good, but no emphasis is placed on speed. We have found on several occasions that a very quick worker finds difficulty

[1] Full information regarding the application of psychology to industry may be obtained from the Institute of Industrial Psychology, Aldwych House, Strand, London, W.C.2.

in demonstrating the job in " slow motion " to new girls, and also tends to be impatient of the laborious efforts and frequent mistakes of her charges. The ideal trainer should combine a high standard of quality in her work with intelligence and finger dexterity. Workroom reports and test records give us the necessary information on her potentialities in these directions. With regard to personal qualifications she must express herself clearly and concisely, have a quick understanding and appreciation of workers' difficulties, a keen interest in human beings and their individual differences, and endless patience.

Trainers are given full responsibility for the initial instruction of groups of new workers ; they begin with an explanation of the arrangement and layout of the work tables, the method of requisitioning materials, recording and checking outputs, and similar details ; they then demonstrate step by step the actual procedure and thereafter follow up and supervise the girls' progress. The time spent in initial instruction is recorded as " demonstration time," and learners receive their wages during this and all training periods.

We have always emphasised with trainers that their greatest responsibility is so to understand and deal with their girls as to promote harmonious relations and ensure thereby that the girls give of their best. Encouraging new workers to improve their efficiency until they have reached the desired standard, requires concentrated effort and attention from those in charge. In the early stages, trainers record, on a blackboard when possible, the hourly output of each girl in the group. When this is not practicable (as in box-making and certain of the manufacturing sections) the time taken by a group of girls for each batch of work is recorded. The importance of hourly records as an incentive in the training of new workers cannot be overestimated. As the trainees become more proficient, daily and, later still, weekly records are adequate.

As stated, the work of the trainers is under the general supervision of a member of the psychological department, who has to ensure that proper layout and methods are being demonstrated by the trainers and that workers undergoing training are improving at the rate that from past experience and learning curves we know to be normal. She has to assist the trainers in every way, where necessary demonstrating actual methods, and advise them in the control of difficult types of girls.

" Incentives and Contentment "

This account of the contribution which psychology has made to the life of the factory would be incomplete if I did not refer to an investigation recently carried out by members of the psychological department and others to throw some light on how a closer degree of co-operation between the management and the workers could be developed. The results of that inquiry have been published,[1] so I need not do more here than briefly state that although I am thankful to say relations between the management and the workers at the Cocoa Works are more than usually cordial, I am satisfied that if we were clever enough to find out how to do it, it should be possible to deepen the spirit of co-operation to the advantage of all concerned.

The inquiry, which covered a good deal of new ground, drew attention to a number of factors which influence the degree of satisfaction in their jobs experienced by the workers. A good many of these are

[1] *Incentives and Contentment : A Study made in a British Factory,* by Patricia Hall, B.Sc., and H. W. Locke, M.A.   Sir Isaac Pitman & Sons Ltd., London, 1938.   2s. 6d.

discussed in this book but the inquiry went, in more detail than I can suitably attempt here, into a consideration of the psychological reaction of the workers to external conditions. The human mind is a very delicate instrument, and he who would play upon it skilfully must be prepared to spend long hours in practice.

Labour Turnover

Before closing this chapter I may suitably add a few words on the subject of labour turnover. I tried in the first instance to prepare some statistics on this subject, but during the last year or two the demand for labour, although on a rapidly rising curve, has been subject to considerable fluctuation, and the directors have hesitated to put men on to the regular staff until there was pretty clear evidence that their employment was likely to prove permanent. I have, therefore, felt it almost impossible to prepare statistics of the actual position which would not be misleading. I may say, however, that in the case of male employees on the regular staff the turnover is only 1·5 per cent. per annum. Of the male employees 607 have over twenty-five years' service, and eighty-six of these have over forty years. In addition to the above, a further 520 have from twenty to twenty-five years' service. It is a rule of the factory that women should leave when they marry, and so, of course, the turnover is higher, being 10·1 per cent.; nevertheless, there are 230 women with twenty-five years of service or more to their credit, and a further 145 have between twenty and twenty-five years. Each year those who have attained twenty-five years' service are presented with a certificate of long service signed by the chairman of the York Board and a gift from the directors, and a social evening is arranged to which they and their wives are invited.

CHAPTER VI

Part I

WELFARE CONDITIONS

WORKROOMS AND CANTEEN

So far the subjects which have chiefly claimed our attention have been the status and remuneration of the workers, their hours of work and the question of their economic security. These constitute the foundation on which the industrial life of the workers is built, and all other matters are secondary to them. Unless the foundations are sound, no satisfactory building can be erected upon them.

I mention this, because it is so important to view industrial conditions in true perspective. Well-designed factory buildings, a good canteen, ample playing fields, efficient medical service, educational facilities, and recreational clubs are all excellent in themselves, but they represent the equipment and decoration of the house of industry. If its foundations are insecure, they will not count for much. But given the sound foundation, these *refinements* of welfare work, if I may so describe them, are of real importance. An unfurnished house, no matter how grand or spacious, is very unsatisfying—and would not be comfortable to live in !

Welfare work of the kind we are here considering has developed so generally since the last edition of this book was published, that I have seriously queried whether there was any object in describing what we are doing in this connection, but I have decided that on the whole it will be worth while to do so. In some directions, many firms are doing better work than we are, but perhaps we may be doing rather better than they in others, so if each of us knows what the others are doing, we can all probably learn something useful. I would, however, advise those whose interest lies chiefly in the fundamental structure of industrial life to skip these chapters and pass straight to the concluding chapter on p. 177.

Factory Buildings and Workrooms

It will, I think, be generally agreed that every employer should seek to surround the workers with the best material environment which his special circumstances and the conditions of his industry render practicable. Clearly, these must vary greatly from factory to factory and industry to industry. One cannot expect to find such good conditions in an old factory in a crowded city as in a new factory in the country, nor can a steel-smelting plant be kept as clean and comfortable as a factory where delicate instruments are assembled. But all employers can place the same aim before them—to make the material working conditions as good as possible.

There are few factories, and I certainly should not include our own among them, where improvements could not be made which would greatly add to the comfort and, incidentally, to the contentment and efficiency of the employees. The fact is that, in the past, employers have not given enough thought to this aspect of business administration. We have regarded our factories as buildings where certain mechanical processes had to be carried out, and the well-being of the workers has often been a secondary consideration.

Let me give a few illustrations of what I mean.

In planning a factory, I suggest that we should aim at some degree of beauty, if that is not too exalted a term to use in this connection. I do not, of course, forget that a factory is built primarily for use and not for show. But so is a cottage, yet a capable architect can design cottages which are not only moderate in cost, and ideally adapted to human needs, but beautiful. Similarly, in factory construction it is worth while to take account of the artistic merit of the design, as well as of its utilitarian merits. If the factory is in the country, and the industry is not one which destroys vegetation, it is easy to beautify a plain building with creepers, such as ampelopsis, which does not require nailing up; while a little space simply laid out, with a few shady trees, makes a delightful spot in which the workers can spend their dinner hour.

Turning now to the workrooms, do not let us regard these merely from the standpoint of machines and processes. Let us remember that men and women or boys and girls are going to spend the greater part of their waking hours in those rooms, and it is a matter of some concern that they should be pleasant places in which to work. A factory architect, if definitely instructed, could do much to render workrooms far more attractive than they often are, without materially adding to the cost of the building. But most of us have to deal with workrooms which are already built, and although we recognise that we might improve on them if building again, the problem is to make the best of what we have. Something can be done by getting good colour schemes for walls and ceilings. Whitewash with a tinge of blue is not prescribed by law! In one department at the Cocoa Works, the attractiveness of a large room has been materially added to by having a green dado on the wall, and the wall area above it washed in a rich cream.

Hanging baskets of plants relieve the monotony of brick walls.

These economical fittings are made of ferro-concrete and non-rusting metal.

Steam pipes below the bottom shelf help to dry clothing in wet weather.

Leaving the æsthetic aspect of the question, all up-to-date factory administrators agree as to the importance of having the workrooms well lighted. I wonder how much eye-strain and headache are caused every day through neglect of this elementary consideration ! Proper ventilation, without draughts, and adequate means to avoid excessive heat in summer and cold in winter are also matters, we shall all agree, which should never be neglected. We know how important they are to us, as we sit in our offices. We cannot do our best if the light is awkward, or if the room is close or draughty, but somehow we are apt to forget that the workers in our factories are just as sensitive to such defects as we are. If we get headaches when the air is " stuffy," so do they, and if we find draughts unpleasant in winter, or catch cold from sitting in them, so do they. In this connection let us give our imagination free play ; and whether our factories are old or modern let us seek to provide conditions in every shop and workroom such as we ourselves should find agreeable and convenient.[1]

Undoubtedly, the provision of good working conditions, and especially the improvement of rooms constructed without due regard to hygiene, will involve a certain amount of expenditure. To some manufacturers this is not a matter of great moment, and they will regard any comparatively small outlay which secures greater comfort for the workers as amply justified. But I would remind any who hesitate on account of the cost, that they cannot expect full efficiency from people who do not work in a healthy and pleasant environment. To improve it is likely to be a wise investment, even from a purely financial point of view. Apart from any other con-

[1] Expert advice on the heating and ventilation of workrooms may be obtained from the National Institute of Industrial Psychology, Aldwych House, Strand, London, W.C.2.

sideration it will attract a better class of workers to the factory. I do not think that our experience at the Cocoa Works in this connection is worth recounting in any detail. We let it be known that we wish to establish thoroughly good working conditions, and we deal promptly with any suggestions or complaints which are made, while the members of the administrative staff are always on the look out for any defect which needs remedying.

Ventilation and Smoke Prevention

We have introduced great improvements in rooms which previously were very dusty, by means of appliances of various kinds for the removal of dust, and we are careful to collect steam from open boiling-pans by means of fans. Much thought is given to ventilation, and wherever this is found to be faulty steps are taken to improve it, often by installing extractors. In some cases considerable improvement results from the provision of fans which merely keep the air in motion without introducing any air from outside. Some of the largest rooms are ventilated on the Plenum system, and air conditions are maintained suitable for both the worker and the product. In winter air is drawn over steam-heated pipes which disperses any fog before the air enters the workrooms, whilst in summer air is passed through a screen of brine-cooled water sprays which at the same time reduces the temperature of the air and filters out any dust which may be in the entering air.

Cloak-rooms and Lavatories

The provision of good cloak-room accommodation is a matter that is often overlooked. From our experience, I suggest the following scheme as satisfactory. The cloak-room should be thoroughly well ventilated, preferably with moving air, so that damp clothes will dry. Hooks should be placed alternately in double rows, one six inches above the other, the distance between them being nine inches. Woodwork should be avoided, and the hooks either attached to metal bars, or bars of ferro-concrete, which we have found cheaper. The bottom row of hooks should be about five feet from the floor, and seven inches from the floor there should be a shelf of perforated metal, with a steam-pipe underneath, so that wet boots may be dried. A similar wire-mesh rack can be provided above the coats for hats. Clothes can be hung on each side of the bar, but in that case the two sides should be separated by expanded metal. An improvement on this (the installation of which, however, is more expensive) is to replace the hooks by metal brackets similar in shape to the ordinary wardrobe coat-hanger. Instead of the coat being bunched together, it is then spread out above the steam-pipe and dries rapidly. At the same time it occupies very little space. This type is shown in one of the illustrations. Of course, the ideal scheme, from the point of view of security, is a steel locker for every worker, but that is very costly, and occupies a large amount of space, besides preventing clothes from drying rapidly. Wherever possible, we keep the cloak-rooms locked, except at starting and stopping times.

As regards washing conveniences, in many cases we provide hot and cold water in the workrooms, and where the workers are handling foodstuffs, the rule is that they must wash after any temporary stoppage before beginning work again. I understand that in some factories a clean towel is provided every time anyone washes. We have not adopted this ideal system, but satisfy ourselves with roller towels frequently changed.

All girls are obliged to provide themselves with overalls and caps of a prescribed pattern. These may be purchased on the factory premises at wholesale prices. The present cost is 4d. for a cap, whilst overalls vary from 2s 10d. to 6s. 3d., the majority of girls paying 3s. 11d. During the past tweve months over 5,000 caps and over 3,400 overalls were purchased. The workers are held responsible for having their overalls washed once a week. For a period we made arrangements at their request for their overalls to be sent to the laundry which serves the factory, and obtained a special contract price of 4d. per overall. This arrangement proved less satisfactory than home laundering, and was terminated with the entire agreement of the workers.

Canteen

Employers are beginning to appreciate, to a much greater degree than formerly, how important a part the canteen plays in the economy of a factory. It is of much less benefit to a man to eat a cold dinner sitting by his machine in the shop where he has worked all the morning, than to eat a hot dinner in a comfortable canteen. Sometimes a director, when very rushed, takes a few sandwiches for luncheon, and eats them at his desk, but he knows that it does not really pay ! It is much better to go away from the office, and have a real break during the luncheon interval. This is just as true of every worker in the factory. But a canteen should be something more than an eating-shop ; it should be a place where the fullest possible advantage can be taken of the dinner hour for the renewal of the vital energy which has been expended during the morning's work.

Whatever may be our special circumstances, whether we are converting a small room in an old building into a canteen, or erecting an entirely new

More than **3,000** workers can be served in the canteen at a time.

elow—
In fine weather girls often spend part of the dinner hour on the lawns. During winter they dance in one of the gymnasia, or go into the theatre, part of whose square roof may be seen in the left background, and where lunch hour entertainments are provided.

building, we should always try to make it thoroughly comfortable. Of course, to secure a good cook is indispensable, but more is needed; the canteen should be a room for the re-creation of strength and energy, and it should be bright and cheerful, since the mind needs refreshment as well as the body. A few plants, or flowers if available, make a wonderful difference, and so do a few pictures. Still more important is it that the tables should be clean; food eaten at a dirty table is never appetising. At the same time, with whatever care a meal is prepared and served, it is difficult to enjoy it thoroughly if one is sitting on a bench with no back! All these facts must be borne in mind, but it would be a great mistake to think that a canteen which fulfilled the above conditions must be palatial. What is needed is not lavish expenditure, but forethought, sympathy, and good sense. It is, of course, important that the canteen service should be quick and efficient.

As to the finance of a canteen, it is necessary at the outset to decide what proportion of the total cost should be met out of the gross profits on the food sold. After a good deal of inquiry as to what has been found possible and desirable elsewhere, we decided at the Cocoa Works to charge prices for the food estimated to cover its cost and the labour incurred in its preparation, also the cost of the service, including the salary of the manageress, the cleaning of the rooms, breakages of crockery, and loss of spoons, etc. The company defrays all other charges—*i.e.* provides and maintains the building and all the equipment, and pays for gas, steam, and electricity.

The present canteen was first opened in March 1914; it occupies the two upper floors of a large three-storey building. On the lower of these there is a room for the girls, which seats 2,400 at tables for eight. The table-tops, which are nineteen inches wide and

I

six feet long, are of eggshell green vitrolite in two
sheets bedded in mastic. The forms have backs,
and can be approached from either end, so that in no
case need a girl pass more than one other person to
get to her place.

The floors are of " Pyrofugent "—one of the many
jointless floor coverings laid down in a soft state,
like concrete. This has proved satisfactory, and, being
red, it makes the room look more cheerful and furnished
than a plain deal floor. If the question of cost did
not arise, however, the ideal would be a floor of
three-inch maple boards ; that is the best covering
for almost all factory floors. It is not, however,
necessary to put a hard-wearing floor in a canteen,
since it is used for so short a time each day.

The men's canteen seats 500. A comparatively
small proportion of men stay at the works for dinner,
as so many live near. Many of the girls, on the other
hand, are the daughters of railwaymen who live
at the other end of the city, or come from adjacent
villages and towns.

There are separate rooms for women clerks and men
clerks, and for forewomen. The few foremen who
stay to dinner dine with the forewomen. In addition
there is a restaurant, where the whole arrangements
and service are similar to those in a good café. It is
open to all who prefer it to the other accommodation
provided, and who are prepared to pay the prices
which are somewhat higher than in the general
canteen. It is used by the directors and executive
officers of all grades, and also by a few rank and file
workers. Anyone is at liberty to bring friends un-
connected with the Cocoa Works. The restaurant
is open every week-day, except Saturday, from 10 a.m.
till 7 p.m. It is largely used for teas, both by people
who are working late, and by those who are staying
at the works for recreation or meetings, or going

thence to engagements in the town. Adjoining it there are lounges with arm-chairs, which form an excellent rendezvous for persons from different departments to meet for conversation.

The canteen building is largely used during the evenings. On Saturday afternoons catering is undertaken for sports clubs, and throughout the winter supper is provided each Friday night for about 200 persons attending the weekly works dances. On other days the various clubs and societies may arrange social evenings and dances, the supper arrangements being made by the dining-room staff.

Almost everything sold in the canteen is " home made." The number of employees using it varies with the weather and the time of year, but the daily average is, roughly, 2,200 women and girls, and 1,500 men and boys.[1] Some buy their whole dinner in the canteen ; others buy something to supplement what they bring from home, while others bring all their food from home, buying only a cup of tea. Any who wish may have the food they have brought from home heated, at a charge of $\frac{1}{2}$d. The time taken in serving the girls is about seven minutes ; the men being fewer in number are served more quickly. The sales during 1936 amounted to about £11,500.[2]

During the summer a large number of workers eat their dinners in the garden. The canteen stands in an old orchard, and both there and in the " Rose Garden " just across the road, seats are provided, though when the weather is fine they seem to be less attractive than the grass. Free meals are provided in the canteen or restaurant for those clerks and administrative officials who are not paid for overtime

[1] The men come to the canteen at different times, according to the shifts they are working, hence a room seating only 500 suffices for their needs.

[2] For a sample day's menu, with the prices charged, see Appendix III, p. 198.

and are working late. On the occasions, usually during the autumn, when the girls work after six o'clock, each is given half a pint of tea free. Free milk during the morning is given to a few delicate employees, on the orders of a works doctor. The cooking in the kitchen is done by steam and gas. We have more than once gone carefully into the question of cooking by electricity, but have ruled the method out on account of its cost.

The whole of the canteen arrangements are under the control of a manageress. She keeps in touch with the wishes of the workers in connection with matters affecting the management of the canteen through an advisory committee appointed annually by the central council. This committee is consulted with regard to any suggested improvement in the service or alteration in the menu. The canteen accounts are submitted to them, and they are consulted as to whether, when the price of materials rises or falls, the situation shall be met by increasing or decreasing the prices charged, or altering the size of the portions. The question has been considered whether the whole management of the canteen could with advantage be placed in the hands of the workers. This is done in some factories, but the plan has not always succeeded, and probably the best canteens in the country are those run by the ordinary administrative staff, with the assistance of a committee of workers.

Part II

RECREATION

That adequate opportunity for wholesome recreation is desirable for all workers, especially in view of the shortening of the working week, will not be disputed. The question is whether an employer has any responsibility in connection with the matter. I think the right answer is that if many of his workers live near the factory he should satisfy himself that adequate recreational facilities exist for them.

He may do this in two ways. Either he may provide adequate recreational facilities for his own employees only, or, by his influence and possibly also his financial help, he may assist communal effort to provide such facilities for the community as a whole. Strong arguments can be brought forward in favour of either course. In the case of a town where voluntary committees or local councils are seeking to provide playing fields, clubs, and similar amenities for the general public, it is certainly a disadvantage if large employers refuse to co-operate in the public effort because they are concerned merely with their own employees. Their attitude might indeed so weaken communal effort as to render action impossible. Again, there are decided advantages in establishing clubs and societies whose membership is not confined to the employees of a single firm. On the other hand, an employer may very well say : " I am prepared to spend thought and money on securing adequate recreational facilities for my own employees, but I cannot undertake the heavier task of ensuring the provision of such advantages for the general public." It is a much easier and quicker process to cater for a comparatively small section of people than to influence public opinion so that measures will be taken which will meet the needs of the whole community. On the whole, I think that the employer should steer a middle course between these two policies. Let him encourage communal effort, and if necessary help it financially, but do not let him rely upon it entirely. Where the public provision is inadequate, and there is no early prospect of changing it, let him see that provision is made for his own workers.

In our case representatives of the company are members of local recreational bodies such as the Juvenile Organisations Committee, and make it their business to know what leisure-time facilities there are in and around the city. Our aim is to see that each evening and on Saturdays there is a fair choice of recreation for every employee, particularly now that we have recently engaged young women and youths from other areas who are away from their homes and acquaintances. This makes it necessary for us to provide quite a number of recreational facilities ourselves. But, apart from other considerations, there are definite advantages in having supplementary work schemes. They often provide opportunities for meeting employees from other departments and belonging to different grades; for instance, social functions at the works are practically the only opportunity for the administrative staff to meet the workers unofficially; thus they help to promote esprit de corps and camaraderie.

Another advantage which we enjoy in providing some of our own recreational facilities is that premises, grounds, and expert coaches and leaders are available at the works. Rooms serving as canteens, classrooms, gymnasia, offices, and so forth during the day are not in use for their ordinary purposes during the evenings and on Saturdays, and the factory buildings are surrounded by lawns, gardens, and fields, of which it would be wasteful not to make full use when playing fields elsewhere are so scarce. The staff of the girls' day continuation school have evening work included in their time-tables so that they can coach juveniles and take classes requiring expert tuition. Besides these there are technicians, craftsmen, and professional people who are willing to give of their expert knowledge, *e.g.* members of the medical staff give talks on physiology and coach our St. John's Ambulance Brigade; joiners take woodwork classes; metal workers conduct art metal-work classes; a painter takes a sketching group; university graduates help in dramatics, literature, music, photography, and in other ways. The goodwill engendered by this generous giving of talents and time by men and women of all grades is of inestimable value to their pupils and the company, and I venture to suggest that it is not without value to themselves. It certainly does much to promote a friendly atmosphere in the factory. I doubt whether this valuable voluntary service would be forthcoming to anything like the same extent for classes not associated with the works.

We have found by experience that there are certain principles which it is important to follow in connection with recreational activities. The first is never to seek to " dump " a club or society on the workers because you think they will like it or that it will be good for them. Of course, there is no need to wait for an articulate demand before doing anything; but begin by suggesting to a few active spirits that it might possibly be a good thing to start a particular club; get them to discuss the idea among their mates, and tell them that if they find the club is wanted you will be willing to help them to establish it. I may add that some of our most successful clubs have been started and carried on without any suggestion and with scarcely any help from the firm. In the case of sports grounds, the company usually looks after these during periods of the year when they are not in use, and hands them over to the clubs ready for use. During the season the clubs look after their own grounds, whether they be football fields, cricket fields, or tennis courts. The clubs also provide their own tackle and meet all running expenses, including such items as the entertainment of visiting teams. The only exception to this virtual independence in the running of clubs is in the case of juveniles who have not yet the experience to shoulder complete responsibility ; they are, however, gradually trained to do so. The administrative and organising experience thus gained is extremely valuable, and it is noteworthy that leaders in recreational activities, either directly connected with the works or elsewhere, frequently reach positions of responsibility in the workrooms.

Another principle which we have found it important to follow is that the company should never become responsible for making good a financial deficit on the working of a club. A representative of the company discusses with the club what contribution, if any, it is reasonable that the firm should make, and after that places the whole of the financial liability on the members. We find that they take much more interest in clubs where financial responsibility rests upon them. If they find that the ordinary subscriptions are not adequate to meet their liabilities, they organise a dance or some social function to make up the deficit. The greater the measure of independence enjoyed by the clubs, the more valuable is the part they are likely to play in the lives of the members. A good illustration of this may be found in connection with the camps. All through the summer months a number of week-end camps, some for boys and some for girls, are arranged in various places near York. Campers go out on Friday evening and return on Sunday evening. At first these were run by members of the social staff, but as the campers became experienced, they developed their own leaders, and now, except in the case of young people under twenty-one, the staff attend camps only when invited to do so by the campers themselves. An example of the independent spirit which has grown up is that of the works company of Sea Rangers, who bought a barge to serve as their camping headquarters, and built two dinghies with money they had raised. These girls take great pride in the fact that they are independent in spite of the heavy recurrent expenditure involved in their enterprise.

Our policy with regard to holidays is to encourage employees to make their own arrangements. Holiday arrangements are, however, made by the company for juveniles who in many cases cannot go away with their own families or friends, and arrangements are made for trips abroad. Young people in particular are encouraged to travel comparatively far afield because of the difficulty the majority will have in doing so when they are married. Endeavours are always made to give the tourists experiences which they would not be likely to get through the ordinary tourist agencies. As far as possible they enter into the life of the people visited, staying on farms, in schools, peasants' cottages, and so on. Arrangements have once or twice been made to use outside tourist agencies, but the workers usually prefer, at any rate in the first instance, to travel with an organiser they know. However, having once been abroad, some of them subsequently join outside parties or go on cruises. Works parties have visited France, Belgium, Holland, Denmark, Spain, Switzerland, Germany, Ireland, and Norway. The trips are entirely self-supporting, except that the company pays the time of the organisers.

About fourteen and a half acres are provided for out-of-door games. In winter there are three grounds available for men's football, also one for men's and two for girls' hockey. In summer there are three cricket pitches, including a concrete pitch, which is much used. There is also accommodation for baseball, which has recently become rather popular. There are four grass and three hard tennis courts, and lawns round the works are used for net-ball and other dinner-time games, and for gymnastic classes and organised games during work hours and in the evenings. Pavilions are provided on the sports fields. Many of our young men are employed on night or shift work, and special care is taken to see that they are adequately provided with sports facilities; the football grounds are in use almost daily, when the weather permits.

Previously, we provided a large number of allotments for the workers, but with the intensive development of housing estates during recent years, in which each house is provided with a garden, we find that the call for allotments is decreasing. They are, however, appreciated by employees who still live in the older types of houses, without gardens. There are sixty-three allotments for male employees. Our experience has been that one-fourteenth of an acre (345 square yards) is about the right size for a man's allotment. Occasionally, a particularly active man will rent two, but this is exceptional. The rents are 10s. a year, including the charge for water, which we have found it necessary to lay on. Seeds, potato sets, manures, etc., are bought co-operatively through the Allotment Holders' Association. A number of allotment holders keep pigs and poultry.

Turning now to the recreational activities which take place indoors, I suppose the most popular of the entertainments are the dances, and not a week passes during the winter when there is not at least one dance. The different departments vie with each other for the credit of having given the best dance of the season.

An activity in which great interest is taken is the Works Dramatic Society, which gives about three performances each winter. Immense trouble is taken in preparing for these, and care is taken to give as many people as possible an opportunity of acting. Notwithstanding the fact that the best actors do not appear in every play, the quality both of the production and acting is often high. The plays are given in a theatre which has recently been erected, which seats 450 people, and is fitted up, from the point of view of seating, stage equipment, and lighting, on lines similar to those of a professional theatre. It is fitted with a cinema projector and sound apparatus, and, in addition to being used for plays, it is used for lectures, concerts, and cinema entertainments. It is occupied practically every night, except in the summer. Reference has already been made to some of the classes held, which might equally well have been described under the section of this chapter dealing with education.

I do not think that any of the other recreative activities call for special comment ; not because they do not fill an extremely useful part in the life of the works, but because they are very similar to those to be found in many other factories. However, I give a list of them in the Appendix,[1] because just as a nurseryman's list suggests to a gardener plants that he would like to see growing in his garden, so some items in this list may be suggestive to those in charge of recreational activities elsewhere.

As far as possible clubs are affiliated to District or National Associations, so that their members may, from the wider contacts made through matches, rallies, and competitions, benefit not only from the point of view of the game or activity involved, but also from the social angle.

In addition to these clubs and societies, which meet regularly, there are seasonal recreational activities, such as sports, swimming galas, Christmas plays, parties for juveniles and for the unemployed, day

[1] See p. 200.

trips, overlookers' week-end excursions, parties to the pantomime or theatre, parties for employees who have completed twenty-five years' service during the year, and an annual " At Home " to members of the central works council. Private parties of employees are also allowed to use the works premises when they wish to celebrate, say, a fellow-worker's twenty-first birthday or coming marriage, and this is greatly valued by those who have not facilities for entertaining in their own homes. The canteen staff is always willing to co-operate to the fullest extent in catering for all these events.

A good deal is done in the way of recreation in the dinner hour. The boys have a dinner-hour club, with table tennis, billiards, and darts ; the girls dance in a gymnasium or spend their recess quietly in a reading and rest room. Concerts and entertainments (given by the employees themselves), cinema shows, table-tennis competitions, and sports are arranged from time to time either in the theatre, the gardens, or in the gymnasia. In the summer many of the employees swim in an adjacent swimming bath presented to the city by the company. With regard to allowing non-employees to become members of clubs, we welcome employees' friends so long as these form a reasonably small proportion of the total number of those connected with any particular activity, and provided they are not keeping our own people out.

Turning now to the question of the cost of providing the recreational facilities, the chief items of expenditure are the fourteen and a half acres of recreation grounds, the theatre, and gymnasia. The theatre is rather a luxury ; it was provided by one of the trusts established by the late Joseph Rowntree. Before it was built the dramatic society performed in one of the lecture rooms, where concerts and other entertainments, now taking place in the theatre, were also given. Apart from the provision of land and buildings, the cost incurred by the company in connection with the various recreational facilities provided amounts to less than £1,000 a year.

The question naturally arises, what is the significance of the activities referred to above ? I think, perhaps, I can answer that question by quoting from a letter sent me by a member of the labour department staff in response to my request for an up-to-date list of the recreational activities at the works. She writes :

" We do not think there is anything important left out. As you will see, we have an enormous variety of activities, and most of them are run by the workers themselves. Our recreational work is not as spectacular as it might be if it were more concentrated and regimented, but we feel it is much better done in our way ; it gives so many people a chance of using their initiative and developing their personalities ; and anyhow, I know amongst the girls, comparatively small societies are much better, as they are so much more friendly, and the individual counts for so much more. I hope we have made it clear what an enormous amount of work is put in by employees for each other ; I always feel it is one of the best things about the works.

" I think our recreational policy is very much in line with the labour policy as a whole, and that it has contributed greatly to the raising of the status of the workers by helping them to be ready to act on their own initiative, and to carry responsibility."

Part III

MEDICAL   SERVICE

Although the provision of a medical service in factories is becoming more general, it does not exist in the majority of even the larger ones. The Association of Industrial Medical Officers only reports forty-three members engaged in whole-time work as factory medical officers. It may therefore be worth while to give some account of the medical facilities provided at the Cocoa Works, and an estimate of their value from the standpoint of the workers and also from that of the management.

The first step in the direction of providing medical services was taken by us in 1904, when arrangements were made for a doctor to attend at the works daily, who could be consulted, without charge, by anyone wishing to do so. After a short time he came to the present writer and said, " If you can't afford to provide both a dentist and a doctor, I advise you to get rid of me and provide a dentist, for so much of the illness is due to faulty teeth that really I think his services are even more necessary than mine." Let me hasten to add that this condition was not due to working in a chocolate factory, for it was just as marked among newcomers as among the older employees ! Later that year a whole-time dentist was appointed, and in 1919 an optician was added to the staff. The total staff now consists of the following :—

(1) A male medical officer, with a woman assistant doctor.

(2) A nursing sister who has had " casualty " experience at a large London Hospital, and three State registered nurses.

(3) A dentist and two dental mechanics, one of

whom is a registered dentist and can thus deputise for the works dentist in his absence.

(4) An optician who attends for two whole days weekly.

The staff also includes a secretary-dispenser, who is responsible for appointments and records, and a typist.

The doctors attend daily from 9.30 a.m. to 5.30 p.m., or at other hours if required. They do not visit the homes of employees.

The medical officers follow, as far as possible, the rules recently suggested by the British Medical Association to safeguard the interests of private and panel doctors. Where temporary medical treatment is not sufficient, the patient's panel doctor is informed.

One of the three nurses spends most of her time in visiting sick employees who have been off work for more than a month. When a large number of employees are engaged on night work, a nurse is detailed for duty at night in the surgery.

In addition to the staff named above, arrangements have been made for an ophthalmic surgeon to examine and, if necessary, treat any cases sent to him by the doctors or optician. The latter refers to him all cases in which the eyes are diseased, or need medical treatment, and which cannot be dealt with simply by the provision of suitable glasses.

The services of doctor, dentist, optician, ophthalmic surgeon, and nurses are free to all employees, as are also any necessary dressings, and sun-ray treatment. The usual charge for a bottle of medicine is 9d., but more is charged if it contains exceptionally costly drugs. All medicines are dispensed in the department. In the dental department patients not eligible for dental benefits under the National Scheme are charged one shilling for a local anæsthetic, and for gas anæsthetics, which are administered by a doctor, from four to twelve shillings according to the extent of the treatment necessary. Artificial teeth are charged for at a price almost equal to the National Health Insurance scale, from £1, 1s. for a single tooth up to £5, 10s. for a full set. In the optical department, the price of spectacles varies according to the prescription for the lenses required and to the style of spectacle frame selected, the most usual price being £1. In the case of both dentist and optician, facilities are given to employees who are members of approved societies to obtain such contributions towards the cost of treatment as their societies give and to pay off the remainder by instalments.

The total net cost of the medical services provided at the works is approximately £4,500 per annum, excluding overhead charges, such as rent and rates, heating, cleaning, and telephone. Before asking whether this expenditure can be justified, a few words may be said about the way in which the department is administered, and the extent to which the employees make use of it.

Anyone wishing to visit the surgery gets a permit slip from the responsible official in his department. This is sent to the clerk in the medical department, who fixes up the appointment. No deduction is made from the day wages of workers for the time spent in visiting the department, but those employed on piece-work lose the difference between what they would have received if working on " day wage " and their piece-work earnings.

Medical Inspection of Applicants for Work

All applicants for work are examined before entrance, or, if for any reason this is not practicable, they must pass the doctor within a fortnight of their appointment. The only significant exception to this rule is made in the building department, where work is of a more casual nature. It may be asked whether it is reasonable to insist on the medical examination of all applicants for work before appointment. If every employer adopted such a course, what would happen to those whom doctors reject ? It is certainly worth while to consider these points. The question whether it is reasonable to insist on examination seems to me to depend on the character of the employment, and the policy adopted towards those who are ill. In discussing the matter with the employees at the Cocoa Works, I have usually put the case in this way. First, we are engaged in the manufacture of food-stuffs, and therefore it is imperative to take all possible precautions. Second, there are about 10,000 workers, including a number of young persons, working in a comparatively small area and mixing freely. It is only fair to those employed, to prevent the introduction of workers who might spread infection. Third, it is an advantage to the workers themselves that they should be examined before starting work. A man is not necessarily rejected because he is suffering from some disease. He may be passed conditionally, *e.g.* as suitable for light work, or work out of doors. It would be much in a worker's interest if, for example, he had a weak heart, to be put on light work, when he might have been put on heavy work if no medical examination had been made. During the last year many youths have been engaged from the Special Areas. Some of these were under-nourished and in poor condition as a result of unemployment. In such cases, at the initial medical examination the youths are passed for light work and during the day shift only, until the general physical condition improves. Occasionally girls are engaged on condition that at first they must be put only on light work, and sometimes they are assigned

K

to remedial classes held in works hours at the company's expense.   In all these cases the medical examination is a distinct boon to the employees.   Lastly, a medical examination becomes almost a necessity if the company is going to accept considerable responsibility for those who break down while in their service.

On p. 74 *et seq.* some account was given of the company's Invalidity Fund.   If all and sundry were engaged, with no medical test, it would be difficult, if not impossible, to accept responsibility for chronic invalids, as their number would probably be much greater than at present, and much stricter regulations would be necessary in the case of those who, though not completely unfit for work, suffer from ill-health and are frequently absent in consequence.

It seems to me, therefore, that there is an overwhelming case for the medical examination of new entrants, always assuming it is carried out reasonably.   But I think the workers may rightly ask that those who pass the test and subsequently break down shall be treated more liberally by the company than they would be were no medical test at entry required.

As regards the second question, as to what would happen to the medically unfit if all employers insisted on medical examination before engaging workers, I do not think this contingency need alarm us.   There are many different kinds of work, and because a man is unfit for one, it does not necessarily follow that he is unfit for another.   If, however, doctors in one employment after another rejected him as unfit for work, surely it would be time to make some special provision for him instead of letting him undertake, for a short time, work at which he could not continue !   The present haphazard policy is clumsy, and a great deal of illness might be avoided by the adoption of wiser methods.

Number of Cases Treated

It is not easy accurately to assess the value of the work undertaken by the medical department. That the facilities offered are appreciated by the workers is proved by the extent to which they take advantage of them. During the year ending 31st December 1937, in addition to the examination of 4,750 applicants for work, the Medical Department received 70,271 visits.

During the same year, there were 4,940 attendances at the dental surgery,[1] while the optician was visited on 1,192 occasions by 787 different persons, to whom 684 fittings were supplied.

Accidents happening when the doctor is absent are treated in the ambulance station, which is in charge of the chief officer of the fire brigade and his assistants, who are qualified ambulance men. The work in a chocolate factory is comparatively free from the risk inherent in such occupations as smelting or heavy engineering work, and we have very few serious accidents.

The doctor periodically examines the hands of those engaged in handling foodstuffs, so as to ensure that no one suffering from any skin disease is engaged in such work. He is also freely consulted on all matters concerning the health conditions throughout the works, and the suitability of different kinds of employment, either for individuals, or for classes of individuals—

[1] The number of attendances at the dental surgery is fewer than that given for the year 1924, when the number of employees was thirty per cent. less than in 1937. This was to be expected. In the initial years dental attention frequently involved extensive treatment needing many visits. These heavy cases have now, for the most part, been dealt with. Regarding the younger members, we have initiated the system of examining and dealing with new-comers, removing all septic and unsavable teeth in one operation. This avoids a number of subsequent visits. Finally, realisation of the value of dental fitness is leading to better care of the teeth, and is reducing the amount of treatment necessary.

e.g. whether any given employment is suitable for women or young persons.

Any worker with a tendency to phthisis is examined periodically until his or her condition is declared to be normal, and all necessary steps are taken to eradicate or, at any rate, to keep in check incipient phthisis. So long as there are symptoms of the disease the worker is, of course, given work where he does not come into contact with foodstuffs. Sometimes employees threatened with it are put to light work, or work out of doors ; sometimes they are sent away for a change of air—a method which may also be adopted in the case of any employee who is run down. There is no doubt that, in not a few cases, the treatment by a doctor of those who show signs of incipient disease has been of the greatest benefit. Sometimes the disease has been completely checked, and in other cases its progress has been greatly retarded. The company has no convalescent home of its own, but the Invalidity Committee takes financial responsibility for sending employees (on the doctor's recommendation) to convalescent homes.

Value of Medical Service

Perhaps a better idea of the value of the medical service than can be gained from general statements may be gathered from a perusal of the results obtained in a number of typical cases. These may be taken as representing what happens throughout the factory.

Medical Cases

(1) A youth had been losing weight and was unable to sleep. His work was poor. An interview with the doctor elicited the facts that he had a cough and " had worried himself stiff " that it was con-

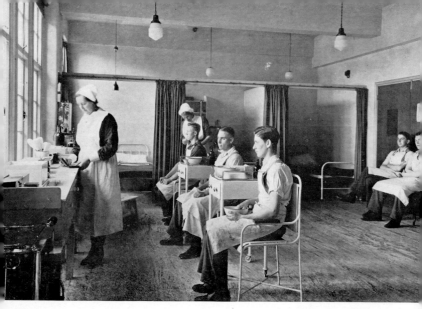

Workers in a light industry do not meet with many serious accidents. Anyone who sustains even a minor injury, either at work or elsewhere, is encouraged to have it dressed in the surgery.

Below—

York is situated in a plain, so bicycles are in popular favour. About 3,500 people come to work each day in this way, and bicycle sheds for this number are provided.

sumption. After a thorough examination he was assured that the cough was of a harmless nature, and after simple treatment and advice rapidly recovered his former health and efficiency.

(2) A boy suffered from anæmia and swollen glands. The doctor was asked to see him. He was given ultra-violet light treatment in the surgery, and outdoor work in the gardens was arranged for him. Great improvement in health and appearance was soon evident, and the boy has been able to keep at work and earn as usual during his cure.

(3) A woman had been in poor health and often lost time on that account. Was persuaded by her forewoman to see the doctor. She soon found herself much improved in body and mind, and wrote saying she regrets that she did not go to him before.

(4) A woman worker who had meningitis in childhood had never been strong. Regular medical supervision and advice by the doctor have enabled her to keep at work and maintain her earning capacity.

(5) A boy had been off work with rheumatic fever. On his return to work, the doctor examined him and arranged for special light work for him, so that he could be earning again long before he was fit to resume his former work.

(6) A boy had been attended by his panel doctor, a competent physician, for headaches and nervous debility, but had made very little progress. The Works doctor visited the boy's workroom and found the work unsuitable for a boy of his temperament. A change of work and a few words of encouragement effected a rapid cure of the trouble.

(7) A caramel boiler with a scalded hand attended the medical department twice daily for dressings and ultra-violet light treatment, and was able to keep at work while his hand was healing.

DENTAL CASES

(1) Woman, aged 30. Before treatment she was constantly off work for odd half-days, and also for longer spells on account of illness. The year before her teeth were extracted she was absent for nine separate half-days in addition to twelve weeks, all these absences being due to ill-health. The year following the extractions, she was never absent from work except for half a day's leave. She states that the serious bilious attacks from which she used to suffer are now much less frequent. She has been promoted, and it is doubtful whether this would have taken place but for her improved health.

(2) Woman, aged 27. Suffered from headaches and inertia. Was surprised to find on consulting the dentist for a minor trouble that she had pyorrhœa. Had all her teeth extracted, and states that now she seldom has headaches or feels debilitated.

(3) Man, aged 49. He states that before dental treatment his " digestion was hopeless," but that now he " can eat anything " ! He maintains that his visit to the dentist was one of the best things he ever did in his life. His manager and overlooker both testify to the improvement in his health and outlook since his teeth were extracted.

(4) A forewoman, aged 38. She went to the optician to have her glasses changed. He suspected an unhealthy mouth, and she consulted the dentist, who found she had pyorrhœa. Her teeth were extracted, and she maintains that since she got rid of the mouth infection which had undermined her health, she has felt much better. She was never absent from work in the year following the extractions.

(5) A woman of 28 whose looks were impaired by decayed teeth. The natural teeth had been filled until they were past redemption, and she stated : " I was

beginning to feel depressed, and colds always went to my mouth." Since treatment she has never been absent from work for more than half a day consecutively, and states : " I feel more lively and think I look better." She has more self-confidence.

(6) A man, aged 24. His manager reports that since his teeth were extracted he seems brighter and more alert. He has been given more responsible work.

(7) A woman, aged 43. She states that before she had her teeth extracted she suffered greatly from abdominal pains. These have now disappeared, and she feels definitely better in her general health.

Optical Cases

(1) Chocolate packer—suffered from headaches daily, and found coloured wrappings particularly trying. Examination by the optician disclosed that though there was little or no optical defect, there was a small degree of muscle balance defect. She was provided with glasses, and has since been able to do her work in comfort.

(2) Applicant for employment—had practically no sight in one eye and would certainly not have been accepted for work. She was seen by the optician, and glasses were ordered, which improved the sight of the bad eye nearly to normal. She has since proved to be a good and useful worker.

(3) Junior worker—had glasses at school, but had discarded them. Had frequent headaches, and her work was poor. The optician found that she had long sight in one eye and short sight in the other. She was persuaded to wear glasses, with excellent results.

(4) Typist—complained of severe headaches, and had been told she did not need glasses as her eyes were good. Examination by the optician disclosed that she was suffering from a muscle balance defect which

prevented the eyes working together perfectly. She attended the ophthalmic department, and was given training to improve the weak muscles. This resulted in a cure without her having to wear glasses.

(5) Chocolate packer—suffered from headaches and " nerves " ; stated that she cried readily, and thought that she could not carry on another day at work. A visit to the optician during working hours disclosed that her eyesight was less than fifty per cent. of normal. Glasses were ordered, and when seen a few months afterwards, she said that she now felt well and able to enjoy work and play.

(6) Girl chocolate maker — had headaches and defective vision. Was fitted with spectacles, and was able to do her work in comfort and with greater efficiency.

(7) Office worker—suffered from headaches. Had not realised that her eyes were defective. Was seen by the optician, and was fitted with glasses, which improved her vision and cured the unpleasant symptoms.

(8) Sales representative—violent headaches, and was almost unable to work. Double vision was confusing. Was found to have a high degree of outward and downward squint. Was fitted with special prismatic lenses, and has since been able to work in comfort.

The optician has been considerably interested in the number of patients who have visited him from time to time, complaining of headache, eye fatigue, etc., which, on examination, were found to be due not so much to defective sight for which glasses were needed, as to varying degrees of muscle imbalance. These muscle defects are often known as latent squint, and prevent the eyes working properly together. The ophthalmic clinic is now provided with special apparatus which enables these cases to be treated by strengthening exercises, which usually result in a cure and the elimination of the need for wearing glasses. The same apparatus is used for the training of many obvious cases of squint. The early diagnosis and treatment of these cases of muscle balance defects are of great importance, particularly as recent work has tended to show that many accident-prone persons have this type of eye defect.

In addition to the service rendered to the workers by the medical department at the Cocoa Works, the labour department encourages workers to join the contributory scheme in connection with the County Hospital. The subscription is 2d. weekly for juveniles between 16 and 20 ; for adults it is 3d. a week, which entitles them and their dependants to free maintenance in hospital. If requested, the subscriptions are deducted from wages. The great majority of those eligible are members of the scheme.

I think the few typical cases recorded above show that the provision of a medical service in connection with a factory is amply justified by the results ; both the employees and the company are benefited. It may, however, be argued that the provision of a medical department is impossible, except in the case of very large factories, and that there are not many such in the country. In many areas, however, it would be possible for several small factories situated in the same area to combine to support a central medical department with a whole-time medical officer. This possibility has not been explored in this country up to the present, but there seems to be no reason why it should not be considered as a means of extending medical supervision to those at present unable to afford it themselves.

Part IV
EDUCATION

The conditions under which industry is carried on to-day are vastly different from those of the " good old days." When businesses were small, and rule-of-thumb methods prevailed, it was easy for employers to maintain intimate relations with their work-people. Furthermore, it was not expected of administrative officials that they should undergo any elaborate training to fit them for their work ; shrewd common sense and practical experience were all that were needed. Those days have gone ; industry is becoming more and more complex, and science is playing an increasingly important part in it. Scientific methods are being used throughout the whole range of business activities. In addition to the older sciences of engineering and chemistry, we now have costing and planning systems, scientific organisation and psychology at our service. An industrial revolution is taking place, and only those who keep abreast of the new methods can hope to succeed. This is particularly true in Britain since the war, for manufacturers are faced not only with home competition, but with the competition of foreign countries, in some of which science is being effectively harnessed to the chariot of industry.

It is by means of these important changes that we may hope to ensure a greater measure of comfort for the community without adding to the hours of work, or to production costs. At the same time the new industrial methods demand a higher standard of education and intellectual application from all workers who fill, or desire to fill, posts carrying a measure of responsibility. To-day most firms are faced with the alternative of bringing their policy and practice into line with world-wide progress or of falling behind in the race.

The adoption of an up-to-date policy will depend on at least two factors for its success ; one is the capacity of its administrative staff to rise to the demands made upon it, and the other is the degree of intelligent understanding shown by the rank and file workers. The education of administrative officials and of the more ambitious or responsible rank and file workers has, therefore, become a necessity in a well-equipped factory. The former have been termed the fourth agent of production. As a result of the increase in the size of businesses, they have come to play an increasingly important part as an intermediary between employers and workers. They have thus the difficult function of interpreting a firm's policy so as to maintain the highest possible efficiency, and at the same time to promote a spirit of goodwill and loyalty in the workers. Leadership is thus an essential quality in an administrator. I venture to think that in the past not enough stress has been laid on the value of the art of leadership when appointing administrative officers, nor have employers been sufficiently anxious to develop that art after their appointment. It has been too often assumed that a thorough knowledge of the technical processes involved was the supreme necessity, and that if this were associated with the power to hustle, little more need be asked. Much of the unrest in industry to-day is due to a lack of tact and of a nice sense of justice on the part of the staff, from charge-hands to directors. They have sought to drive when they should have been leading, and they have been satisfied with rough justice instead of insisting on as complete justice as possible in each case. The somewhat rough-and-ready method of handling labour which has so often done duty in the past will not serve us in the future, any more than will the old rule-of-thumb industrial processes where science is ignored and costing systems are unknown. Both are becoming relics of the past. Just as we must give science a more prominent place in the development of industrial processes, so we must learn to handle the human problems of industry with more intelligent sympathy and tact. We must induce men to do their best by encouragement, inspiration, and example.

But here we are face to face with a practical difficulty. It is comparatively easy to find foremen with good technical qualifications and the capacity to " hustle," but it is difficult to find men who can inspire and lead. Yet such men must be found or made, for the plain fact is that workmen nowadays refuse to be driven. Unless we can learn to lead them industry will suffer severely. I suggest, therefore, that those responsible for the administration of business should realise the great importance of surrounding themselves with a body of administrative officers possessing not only the necessary technical qualifications but the power of leading men. Obviously the first essential in securing this end is to select for administrative posts those men who, besides the necessary technical qualifications, have tact and sympathy. But that is not enough. They should be told quite clearly what are the ideals of the directors as to the way in which the business should be administered, and the relations which should be established and maintained between the management and the men. Emphasis should be laid on the need for absolute justice and the importance of courtesy, and a high ideal held out regarding the part which a foreman or other officer may play in creating a right " atmosphere " in the works. The great changes which have come over industry during the past few years should be explained, and the staff made to realise how much greater are the claims made upon it now than formerly.

Training of Administrative Staff

At the Cocoa Works, while we have not overlooked the importance of providing for the potential administrative staff of the future, we have been concerned mainly with the training of the existing staff. We have at one time or another tried the following schemes :—

(1) Lecture courses and conferences at the Cocoa Works.

(2) Attendance at lecture conferences dealing with industrial questions, held at Balliol College, Oxford, and elsewhere.

(3) Travel groups.

(4) Staff magazine.

1. *Lecture Courses at the Cocoa Works.*[1]

These are of two kinds : the courses in theory and practice of administration, and the more general courses in educational subjects, such as Economics, History, Psychology, English, and so on. The first experiment in the way of lectures on administration was made in 1919, when twelve lectures were given during working hours by directors and heads of departments to the whole of the administrative staff. Similar courses in administration have been given to members of the staff since then, but usually after working hours.

As modern methods of management came to be adopted in the Works, we found the need for some method of explaining the reason for their adoption and the way in which they would affect foremen. After discussion with the overlookers' committee, we decided for this purpose to organise a special series of

[1] The organisation of all educational work throughout the factory is undertaken by a whole-time education officer. See p. 166.

conferences to be held during working hours. The foremen and forewomen were divided into three groups, each group attending once a week ; this meant, in effect, that the conferences were repeated three times weekly with the different groups. A printed text, dealing with the subject-matter, was prepared by the appropriate official under the general editorship of the firm's education officer. These texts were simple, concise statements of the firm's policy and practice, giving a fairly detailed explanation as to why these had been adopted. The texts were distributed a week in advance of the conference, and the foremen were asked to read them in the interval. Each conference was under the leadership of the official whose function was being considered.

The actual conference subjects which were dealt with were as follows :—

> The Policy of the Company.
> The Organisation of the Company.
> Organisation for Production.
> Time Study and Rate Fixing.
> Wages Policy and Wage Systems.
> Psychological Tests at the Cocoa Works.
> The Human Factor.
> Personnel and Social Work.
> Time-keeping.

Our aim in preparing these documents was to provide something which the overlooker could regard as authoritative and instructive, and which would explain to him why certain lines of action had been laid down. The manual included general instructions to overlookers, with a statement of their duties, and showed how these were linked up with the whole organisation. The labour involved in this experiment in training overlookers was considerable, but we felt that it had been well worth while, and had most beneficial results in the workrooms.

We found conferences much more successful than lectures in evoking an active and critical attitude. It must be remembered that the general education of the average foreman has hardly developed since he left school many years ago, and that he is of an age when ordinary educational subjects have little attraction for him personally. He is, however, intensely interested in his job and in anything likely to help him to do it better. He is keen to get better and cheaper production, and his interest in this aspect of business can be made the peg on which to hang the training programme. To be successful any such programme must be whole-heartedly supported by the higher management and put over with the spontaneous co-operation of the foremen themselves. At all costs must the notion be avoided that the foremen are being sent to school again, nor must the idea get about that the plan is being adopted because the present staff are not up to their jobs.

2. *Lecture Conferences.*

We have taken advantage of the series of conferences of directors, works managers, and foremen which, for many years, have been held during vacations at Balliol College, Oxford. Their main purpose is to help industrial administrators to meet the new conditions in industry to which reference has been made above. It has been a great help for our foremen and others to mingle at these conferences with administrative officials from other factories and to listen to addresses on some of the larger problems of industry. Employers are a little apt to forget how few opportunities most executives enjoy of enlarging their ideas on industrial matters, particularly in an isolated provincial town with few industrial traditions. They seldom travel, or have any chance of hearing how others are dealing with the problems which they have to face every day. If we do not give them the opportunity to enlarge their ideas, we cannot blame them if they get into a rut and fail to grasp the changes which are so rapidly coming over industry. At these conferences, to which any firm may send representatives, much attention is devoted to the human side of business administration.[1] The character of the subjects dealt with may be gathered from the following programme of a conference held at Balliol College, Oxford :—

35TH OXFORD MANAGEMENT CONFERENCE

(for Directors, Managers, and Supervisory Staff)

BALLIOL COLLEGE   24th to 28th September 1936

SYLLABUS AND PROGRAMME OF LECTURES

" The Planned Progress of an Individual Business "

Thursday, 24th September.

6.30 p.m.   Reception in Junior Common Room.

8.0 p.m.   Professor Noel F. Hall.

A Survey of the economic probabilities to be considered in planning the future of a business ; the help an economic adviser can properly give an industry or a company on major questions of policy, the report he would submit on the relevant conditions during the period with which the company's plan would be concerned.

Friday, 25th September.

10.0 a.m.   Mr. A. P. M. Fleming.

Controlling the growth of organisation necessitated by the company's policy. " Bridging the gap " from the abstract idea to the marketable product, through the stages of research and development up to the production stage ; the broad features of production and distribution which must be appreciated before a plan is made ; the alignment

---

[1] Full particulars of these conferences may be had from Mr. Reginald Pugh, Confederation of Management Associations, Terminal House, 52 Grosvenor Gardens, London, S.W.1.

planned industrial activity.

Afternoon. Visits to local factories.
8.0 p.m. Dr. J. A. Berger.
>Market research ; an investigation of the markets available for the product chosen whether the product be a consumption or a production commodity.

Saturday, 26th September.
10.0 a.m. Mr. Sinclair Wood.
>The formulation of a long-term sales policy as suggested by the research.

4.45 p.m. Mr. D. L. Armstrong.
>The public relations and advertising campaign ; promotion of goodwill, and generally the preparation of the right atmosphere for the reception of the plan by the public, whether the public be a consumer public or a producer public.

8.0 p.m. Mr. B. S. Rowntree.
>The determination by the board of directors of the policy and purpose of the business.

Sunday, 27th September.
2.0 p.m. Mr. E. D. A. Herbert.
>The basic production plan of a business, including the progressive extension of plant ; adoption of new methods ; supply of technical staff and labour ; and the general tuning-in to the sales objective.

4.45 p.m. Mr. R. J. Dowdell.
>An appropriate long-term policy of purchasing and stock-control ; supply of materials, and a systematic handling of forward deliveries.

8.0 p.m.
>The relation between the progress of an individual business, and public opinion and needs.

Summing-up by the Chairman—Dr. C. H. Northcott.

Monday, 28th September.
>Break up of Conference.

3. *Travel Groups.*

The disadvantages from which the lower grades of the administrative staff suffer in not being able to

L

travel and meet men from other firms were mentioned in the preceding paragraph. Our scheme of travel groups was an attempt to meet the need. On several occasions in the past the Overlookers' Associations had organised day trips to certain industrial centres and to works. In 1922 we tried a new and more ambitious experiment. A series of four tours was arranged, which included visits to a number of important factories in and near London. Each tour lasted four days, and ended with a day at Cambridge, where the party, which numbered about twelve, was entertained by members of the University. At the end of each day the party met together under the leadership of our education officer (who conducted the tours) and discussed the various points arising out of the day's visit. This experience was undoubtedly successful, and I regret that circumstances made it impossible to repeat it in subsequent years. We have, however, for many years now during the spring and summer months arranged a series of one day visits to other works for groups of our foremen and fore-women. In this way factories have been visited in Manchester, Newcastle, Birmingham, Hull, and Leeds. The value of such visits is not so much in seeing how other things are made as in finding out how other firms handle workroom problems, such as those related to planning, processing, breakdowns, discipline, and so forth.

4. *Staff Journal.*

For two or three years we published a Staff Journal which was distributed free to every member of the administrative staff. Its aim was to keep the officials informed of developments in the business world and other matters likely to help them in their work. The journal was not published at stated intervals, but usually appeared three or four times a year. Pressure of other work on those responsible for preparing it has led to its suspension, but there is a need for something of this kind in a large factory where the central policy of the directors is apt to get lost in a mass of departmental details. Discord and friction are often traceable to ignorance on the part of officials of the firm's policy or of certain matters affecting the internal organisation, but the facilities of the Technical Library (to be explained later) have been extended, and now administrative officers have their attention drawn to any articles in business journals which are likely to be of special interest to them.

General Education

I come now to the question of general education in the factory. This includes the provision of facilities for adolescents and for adults.

Girls.—Classes for girls, held during working hours, were begun in 1908. At first these occupied three hours, and attendance was obligatory for all girls who were under seventeen when they came to the works. They attended until the end of the term, during which they reached the age of eighteen, or for three years, whichever was the shorter. Various domestic science subjects were taught, as well as gymnastics and English.

In 1921 it was announced that the York Education Authority was going to open a continuation school providing much the same kind of instruction as we were giving, and we therefore decided to close our school and, for the time being at any rate, to allow the Local Authority to use our classrooms. Unfortunately, the proposals did not materialise, so we restarted our school, but only for two hours a week and for girls up to sixteen.

The girls now have an hour of gymnastics and an hour of English weekly. The gymnastic training includes swimming and organised games such as netball, whilst the term " English " is very widely interpreted in accordance with our policy of linking up the class work with leisure time interests and activities. Instruction has also been given in group-singing and hygiene. Girls are encouraged to attend voluntary evening classes in domestic science given in the city.

For the year ending 31st December 1937, the cost of the Girls' School as described above, with an average of about 700 on the books, was as follows :—

Salaries and Teachers' Superannuation Fund . .	£1,326
Wages paid for the time at classes	221
Supplying shoes and supplying and washing gymnastic costumes	164
Books and other equipment	30
Pianist for gymnastic classes	23
Lighting, heating, and cleaning (including caretaker) .	390
Rates, repairs, depreciation, and insurance . . .	123
Travelling and sundry	21
Rent (5 per cent. on written down capital cost of premises and fittings)	115
	£2,413
Less Government Grant . . .	1,100
Net cost	£1,313

It will be seen that the cost works out at about £2 per girl per annum.

Boys.—Classes for boys were started in 1905. All boys from fourteen to seventeen attended for six hours a week, four of which were in work time. The curriculum included physical training and gymnastics, mathematics, English, and woodwork, experimental physics and chemistry. The four teachers were also responsible for supervising the social activities organised for boys in their leisure hours, such as games, week-end camps, and evening clubs.

The girls and boys attend physical culture classes each week during working hours.

Below—In fine weather these classes are held on the lawn.

These classes were closed in 1915, as the teachers were called up for military service, and were not reopened, for the same reason that we closed the girls' schools. At the request of the central works council, the gymnastic classes were restarted in 1920, the boys attending for one hour a week. The cost of these classes, including a charge for rent of the rooms used, was £776 for the year ending 30th June 1937. The average number of boys attending was 526.

In the latter half of 1937, the directors agreed to co-operate with the York Education Committee in the establishment of a voluntary day continuation school for boys employed by local firms. Under this new scheme all boys employed by the company between the ages of fourteen and seventeen inclusive will go to the school for one continuous session of four hours (one-half day) per week in the company's time, and also for two hours in their own time. The school is organised and staffed by the York Education Authority which, consequently, bears the full cost of administration, salaries, and equipment. The company, however, pays wages at the standard time rate for the half day spent by the boys at school. The curriculum is very similar to that of the classes which were held at the Cocoa Works between 1905–15. Though the school is open to all boys employed by local firms, at the present time the pupils come entirely from the Cocoa Works.

Adult Education

I now pass to a brief description of the steps taken at the Cocoa Works to encourage adult employees in general to continue their education.

Organised effort in the direction of providing general adult education dates from 1920, when two reasons led us to systematise and develop facilities for it. One was a growing demand from a section of the workers, and the other a recognition on the part of the directors that a high general standard of education was essential to the industrial efficiency demanded by modern conditions. We therefore appointed an education officer to supervise this work.

He began by attending meetings of all the departmental councils throughout the works, and spoke of the importance of education and of the help which he was prepared to give. Each department elected two representatives to discuss the matter with him. This was the first step towards creating the atmosphere required and towards focusing educational enthusiasm, otherwise scattered and ineffective. These departmental representatives became the normal means of bringing matters of educational interest to the notice of employees. It was then made known throughout the works that the education officer's services were at the disposal of anyone who wished to take up a course of study, either by attending classes or by private reading. Arrangements were made to enable anyone in the works to go to his office during working hours for advice. He, in turn, was to keep in close touch with the Local Education Authority and bring to its notice the special needs of Cocoa Works employees. This method of encouraging adult students to attend classes organised by the Local Education Authority has not been entirely satisfactory, even where they have been specially arranged for our employees. This is due partly to their dislike of going to a school, and partly to the fear of being mixed with juniors and outsiders before whom it is disagreeable to display ignorance. It is much better to have classes taken by members of the staff known to the men and women individually, and for these reasons the education officer, aided by a committee appointed by the central works council took, in 1922, the further step of providing a number of classes at the Cocoa Works for adult workers in general. In organising these courses they kept in view the needs of the adult student who was rather out of touch with educational topics. The teaching was as informal and practical as possible, and many of the classes were held in the café lounges. All of the lecturers were qualified men and women, and most of them were Cocoa Works executives. In the winter of 1936–37 about 650 employees attended the works classes and lectures.

The principal items in the programme for that year were as follows :—

(1) A course in industrial management, open to all employees, but attended mainly by the more enterprising of the younger junior executives. The syllabus for this particular year covered a variety of subjects connected with the function of marketing.

(2) Training course in the duties and work of a private secretary.

(3) English course for typists.

(4) Course on modern industrial and social history.

(5) A course on musical appreciation. (Courses (4) and (5) were given by the Workers' Educational Association.)

(6) A University Extension Course on dramatic art.

(7) A series of open evening lectures and lunch-hour discussions on current affairs.

(8) A course of six meetings for shop stewards.

There were also :—a special course for the factory employees, mostly girls, who act as visitors' guides ; a class on sketching, painting, and design ; courses for men in first-aid ; a course for youths who desire to increase their facility in everyday calculations and in expressing themselves in speech and writing.

In addition to the above, a good many activities of

the type usually associated with clubs are fostered. For some years we had a definitely organised girls' club run by a member of the social staff, but, two or three years ago, when the growing number of girls made it necessary to enlarge the staff of our girls' continuation school, evening classes were organised under the expert instruction of the school staff in most of the subjects touched upon by the girls' club, which was therefore discontinued. The girls now have the choice of the following classes, or group activities carried on independently : physical training, dressmaking, handicraft, first-aid, and home nursing classes ; sports, sketching, rambling, and dramatic clubs, as well as concert parties and numerous dances and other social events. Except in the case of the youngest employees, and classes coming under the Board of Education, these activities are self-governed. The company provides the necessary grounds or indoor accommodation and, where necessary, the staff.

Training of Clerical Staff

The present scheme was drafted by the company in 1931 and agreed to by the National Union of Clerks. Specific standards of proficiency were established, and clerks were required to attain these, taking advantage of classes arranged on the company's premises, as described above, or available in York, or working privately for the examinations required. All candidates for clerical employment must have reached the age of sixteen years. They are required to pass an entrance examination designed to test both innate ability and knowledge of general educational subjects. If over eighteen years of age, they may also be required to pass a test in technical subjects such as shorthand and typewriting. The female clerical staff is divided into three grades :—

(1) General clerks and machine operators.
(2) Shorthand typists.
(3) Comptometer operators.

New girls are allocated to the grade for which they have shown aptitude in the preliminary tests, or for which they have a special preference. By the time they have reached the age of twenty, female clerks are required to obtain the following qualifications in the particular branch of clerical work to which they have been allotted :—

(1) General Clerks and Machine Operators.

Royal Society of Arts Intermediate Certificates in English, Arithmetic, and two other approved subjects.

(2) Shorthand Typists.

The company's Grade 2 Shorthand Typists' examination, consisting of the following tests :—

    (a) Knowledge of English language (two hours' paper).

    (b) Speed tests—shorthand, 100 words per minute ; typing, 50 words per minute.

(3) Comptometer Operators.

The comptometer diploma of Messrs. Felt & Tarrant.

(4) Alternative Training.

General clerks and machine operators who wish to undertake comptometer training, but are not engaged on comptometer work, may only do so at the discretion of the Staff Office, and after having obtained two Royal Society of Arts certificates, in English and Arithmetic. Should they fail to make satisfactory progress during their first year of comptometer training, they are then required to complete the standards required from them as general clerks and machine operators, but are allowed one extra year to do so.

Members of the clerical staff who fail to reach the required standard of proficiency by the age of twenty are debarred from applying for posts advertised by the company except by permission of the Staff Office.[1]

Special standards are required for shorthand typists and for secretaries; the subjects of examination for these are :

(1) Grade 1.—Shorthand Typists.

  English—two hours' paper (approximately equivalent to London Matriculation standard) testing :
    Spelling.
    Précis writing.
    Punctuation.
    Business correspondence.
    Vocabulary.
  60 per cent. marks constitute a Second Class, 70 per cent. a First Class pass in this grade.
  Shorthand, 120 words per minute.
  Typing, 60 words per minute.

(2) Secretarial Certificate.

  Part I. Two papers covering the preparation of reports and summarising of correspondence, English grammar and construction, and letter writing.

  Part II. Two papers of :—
    (a) General and business knowledge, including filing, indexing, and use of reference books ; and

---

[1] It was stated on page 102 that it is the practice of the company to advertise in the works any administrative and minor executive posts.

(*b*) Arithmetic, including problems, percentages, elementary statistics, and graphs.

All questions are related as closely as possible to the business and organisation of Rowntree & Co. Ltd. ; the required standard of written work is approximately that of London Matriculation.

Part III. Shorthand, 120 words per minute.
Typewriting, 60 words per minute.

Male clerks are expected to reach certain minimum requirements by their twenty-fifth year. These include advanced certificates of the Royal Society of Arts in five subjects, as follows :—

(1) Commerce ;
(2) Economic Theory or Economic Geography ;
(3) Book-keeping, or French, or Spanish ; and
(4) Two other subjects approved by the education officer of the company.

Clerks who pass the Inter. B.Comm. of London, the Final Examination of an approved professional association or institute, or any equivalent examination approved by the education officer of the company, are exempt from these minimum requirements.

All junior clerks are interviewed by the company's education officer not only on engagement but regularly during the whole period of their training, with regard to their courses of study and the progress made. For general commercial subjects, clerks are advised to attend the local Institute of Commerce, but special reasons have induced us to hold classes at the Cocoa Works in touch typing, shorthand, comptometer operating, and English.

TECHNICAL TRAINING

In addition to the schemes outlined above, we have at the Cocoa Works a special scheme for technical apprentices. Although we are primarily neither an engineering nor a building concern, we have a comparatively large staff of technical workers, and a number of apprentices, who are trained under a special scheme. This includes five to seven years' practical instruction in the shops in all branches of their particular trade, together with a definite course of training at the local technical institute, leading up to the recognised examinations, such as the Higher National Certificate in engineering or building. The apprentices attend at the local technical institute for one-half day a week in works time and for two evenings. Their wages are paid for the time lost from work, and they are further encouraged by the award of prizes to those who are successful in their examinations, and by the refund of class fees to all who attend regularly throughout the session.

Libraries

Our educational work is supplemented by two libraries, the " Joseph Rowntree Library " and the Technical Library. The former is for the use of all employees, and is stocked with fiction and general literature. It contains about 26,000 volumes. It is open daily, except on Saturdays and Sundays, from 12.30 p.m. to 2 p.m., and for half an hour after leaving time. Employees have free access to the shelves and may handle the books, and the librarian is always willing to help them to choose suitable ones. The librarian is advised by a library sub-committee of the central works council, and has endeavoured to make the library of the widest possible use in the works by

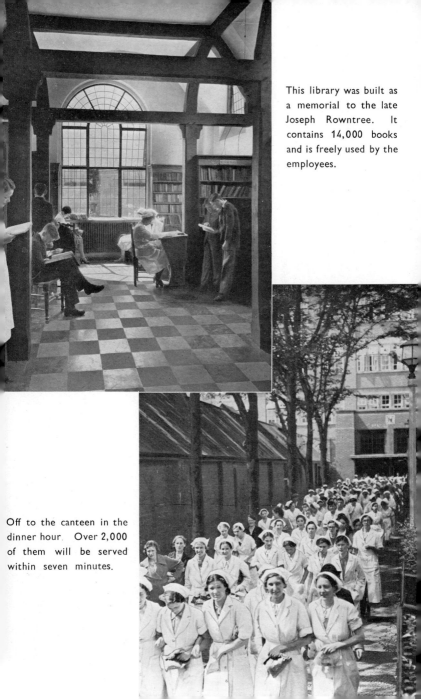

This library was built as a memorial to the late Joseph Rowntree. It contains 14,000 books and is freely used by the employees.

Off to the canteen in the dinner hour. Over 2,000 of them will be served within seven minutes.

catering for different tastes in literature. About 1,000 books are borrowed weekly, of which approximately ninety per cent. are fiction. The library houses also the private library of the late Joseph Rowntree, and a reading-room in which employees are able to study with reference books at hand.

The Technical Library deals entirely with subjects coming within the scope of our business. In addition to functioning as a library, it acts as an information bureau and intelligence department. A staff of four is engaged in selecting and indexing all relevant periodical and other literature likely to be of interest to persons engaged in different branches of our business. Bulletins are circulated amongst administrative officers, drawing their attention to matters which concern them.

About 120 periodicals are read, and a large number of pamphlets, Government and other reports. A careful look out is kept for books likely to prove of value to the business. The technical library is made available to all employees who attend works classes.

Works Tours

One final matter which can, I think, be properly mentioned under the heading of education is the arrangement made for employees to be shown round the works. Groups of six or seven workers make the tour under the guidance of a suitable member of the staff, who explains the work of the various departments and how the processes are linked up to the work of those making the tour. It is believed that in this way employees are given a greater interest in the work as a whole and in their own work in particular. The trend of industry is all in the direction of specialisation, and this in turn tends to give the individual worker a somewhat narrow and uninteresting outlook. The tours are an attempt to counteract this by giving them the opportunity to see something of the organisation as a whole, and thus enlarging their interest in the firm. In addition to these tours of our own works, it has been our practice for many years to arrange for parties of our employees to visit other factories in or near York on Saturday mornings. Such visits are greatly appreciated.

RESULTS OF THE EDUCATIONAL WORK

It will be seen from the foregoing that we have tried to cater in some measure for the educational needs of the several grades and ages of the working force at the Cocoa Works. The question may well be asked— what results have been achieved ? In answering this question we must be clear as to what we mean by the word "results." It usually suggests something quantitative rather than qualitative, and, in any case, something which can be measured. The results of educational work are seldom immediately visible, and, though probably far-reaching, may be very indirect. Dealing first with the administrative staff training, I am convinced that much valuable work has been done amongst large numbers of our officials and especially the overlookers. The tendency to drift and to be content with the good old methods has been checked. The consciousness of the new conditions in industry is fairly general, and in many cases the heavier demands made on the staff are being successfully met. One indirect result which has been wholly good is that the various grades of the administrative staff have been brought into closer touch with one another. By means of the lectures given by the heads of functions, and the discussions which followed, the overlookers have learned a great deal of the firm's policy, aims, and difficulties, whilst the lecturers themselves have come to know something of the difficulties which have to be faced by the overlookers in the workrooms. The scheme for the training of clerical staff has, I think, been successful. The standard of attainment of our clerks of both sexes has been raised to a high level during the past fifteen years.

I cannot speak so definitely of the effects of the general adult education scheme, as there is less data on which to base an opinion. One piece of evidence as to the value of the scheme is to be found in the large percentage of employees who, having once begun, have attended for two or more years. Another is the statement made by several of our students that through our classes they have been encouraged to take an interest in the education of their children. Finally, it must be remembered that the more educated workers tend to leaven the ideas of the rest.

I have already referred to the value of the gymnastic and swimming classes in improving the boys' health and physique. Equally beneficial results have come from the girls' physical training, and this must inevitably be of advantage not only to the girls but also to the company. As regards the other teaching given to girls, I have no doubt it benefits the girls, but it would be difficult to bring forward concrete evidence that it directly benefits the company. It certainly tends to raise the general tone, and, as one of several amenities, it attracts a better class of workers. It also draws attention to particularly capable juniors who are encouraged to take advantage of further educational facilities provided in the works or in the city. But from the purely industrial standpoint it can hardly be expected that the provision of educational facilities for all the young girls will directly pay the particular firm that provides them. This is not an argument against their provision ; it merely means that the direct benefits are communal rather than industrial.

With the boys the situation is different. It is impossible to speak with certainty, but I am inclined to think that the education given to the boys is not only an advantage to them but also to the company. In making this statement, I bear in mind that a number of the lads will remain with us throughout their working lives, and that many of these have become more alert, observant, and efficient, and have gained a higher ideal of their duties as workers and as citizens through the school influence. This is an industrial asset of real value.

CHAPTER VII

SUMMARY AND CONCLUSIONS

Summary

It only remains now briefly to summarise what has been said in the preceding chapters, and to assess the significance of the various developments in labour policy there described. Dealing first with the workers' status, over a long period of years, we have been experimenting with a view to seeing how far it was possible to adopt democratic methods in connection with all matters directly affecting the workers, and it has been shown in the chapter dealing with the workers' status that we have gone a long way in that direction.

Every works rule (and it is these rules which regulate the conditions of work) has been jointly approved by the management and the workers, and no rule can be altered and no new one made except by joint agreement. No foreman can be appointed except after discussion between the shop steward and the manager of the department concerned. The management has renounced the right to be the ultimate judge in disciplinary matters. Any man who has been subjected to disciplinary action for a breach of a works rule can appeal against any punishment inflicted, to an impartial appeal committee whose decision is final. We have never had cause to regret our action in this matter, nor has it lowered the standard of discipline throughout the factory.

Previously, we had maintained that as employers we had the right to the last word in matters of discipline, as is the usual practice, but as a matter of fact it is contrary to the tenets of justice that matters of this kind should be decided by an interested party. We do reserve the right to dismiss or demote men for matters directly concerned with their work, such as continued carelessness or inefficiency or idleness. This, I think, must always rest with the management, but in our case if a foreman wishes to dismiss a man for any reason, the dismissal must first be approved by the manager of the department, and next by the labour department. It may be remembered that the chief shop steward is a member of the staff of that department, and no dismissal takes place until it has been submitted to him, unless it has already been agreed to by the shop steward in the department concerned. Thus it would be almost impossible for an employee to be dismissed without adequate cause. The foremen know this quite well ; indeed, I think some of them feel that our precautions against unjust dismissal are excessive, and that so many formalities have to be completed before a man can be dismissed that they hesitate to take action in certain cases where they would like to do so. There is probably a measure of truth in this, but it is not a heavy price to pay for the assurance that no unjust dismissals take place. It follows from what I have said that we could never have labour unrest or a strike because the workers thought that a man had been unfairly dismissed, and how many strikes occur every year just for this very reason !!

Another step in the democratisation of management is giving the workers full opportunity to raise with the management any questions which they desire to do. We have adopted various steps in this connection. First, we have councils in the different departments which meet as often as is found necessary, and a central council for the whole works which is supposed to meet monthly, but which, in fact, only meets about eight times a year, because more frequent meetings have been found to be unnecessary. The central council consists of thirty workers' representatives elected by the workers, and twenty-six representatives of the administrative staff, always including two or three directors. The chairmen of the councils are selected from the administrative and the workers' sides of the council alternatively, and hold office for two years.

Any question which is of general interest may be raised at these meetings by anyone present, but the council does not discuss individual complaints which should be settled by other means. Nor does it discuss the basic wage rates, hours of work, and length of holidays; these are negotiated with the trade union and the Interim Industrial Reconstruction Committee.

Periodically, the chairman of the York board of directors addresses the council on the progress of the business. He tells them about sales in the different departments, about any special advertising campaign that may be contemplated, and of the various efforts which are being put forth to advance the interests of the business. He tells them of any special difficulties with which the business may be confronted, and generally gives them the kind of information which should be given to the workers if they are asked to co-operate with the management in running the business successfully. These addresses often give rise to useful discussions. After these addresses the council members may ask any questions they wish, and make any criticism they desire of the management. This liberty does not lead to mere grumbling. Criticisms are made in a constructive spirit. A meeting is held every year at which the chairman of the York board of directors, or the labour director, meets the whole of the shop stewards merely to answer any questions they wish to ask him. The chief shop steward presides at this meeting and encourages those present to be perfectly frank in asking anything they wish ; and finally, a meeting open to any worker who likes to attend is held once a year at which a full account of the year's trading is given and questions are encouraged. Thus it will be seen that ample opportunity is given to the workers to express their views and to obtain information with regard to the working of the business.

All the arrangements described above are now working smoothly, and to the advantage of all concerned. They have not lowered the standard of efficiency or of discipline, but I think it will be admitted that under such an organisation the status of the workers is that of co-operators and not that of servants.

Passing now from status to other matters, and dealing first with wages, we have seen that these are fixed at the Cocoa Works by negotiation between the unions and the employers. Basic conditions affecting wages, hours, and holidays are determined by the Interim Industrial Reconstruction Committee and apply to about forty per cent. of the workers in the industry, membership of the council being optional. The wages fixed by this council are substantially higher and the working conditions better than the statutory minima which are determined by the Trade Board.

There are one or two other matters which closely affect the workers' earnings, which may possibly be of general interest. First, the use of psychological methods in the selection and training of workers. I can say, with confidence, after many years' experience, that the value of these methods in selecting young workers has been amply proved. It has reduced the proportion of misfits from about twenty per cent. to five per cent. To assign workers to jobs for which they are temperamentally suited not only adds to their contentment but also to their earning power. The use of psychological methods in the training of workers has materially shortened the learning period, which is, of course, an advantage to all concerned.

Another matter in connection with wages to which I may here refer is that the shop steward has the right *ex officio* to attend a time study—a right scarcely ever exercised. He does, however, satisfy himself that the conditions under which the test is conducted are such as would normally be adhered to in practice, and it is this knowledge of the circumstances that enables him to discuss the fairness of the rate with the time-study investigator. This responsibility is vigilantly exercised.

No piece rate becomes operative till both the management and the workers (through their shop steward) have agreed that it is fair. A guarantee has been given that no piece rates shall be reduced once they are fixed unless the conditions of work have changed or it can be shown that a mistake was made when fixing them. Whenever a change is found to be necessary it is made in co-operation with the workers ; it is never imposed on them.

I believe that every industry should pay the highest wages which it can afford, having regard to the fundamental importance of maintaining the business in a financially sound condition and establishing adequate reserves. This has been the policy which we have pursued, but in wage negotiations it is necessary to observe due prudence in the wages which it is agreed to pay. It must be remembered that when one is agreeing to a scale of wages, one is banking on profits which have yet to be earned. It may, however, be that these turn out better than anticipated. In such case, half of any surplus profits [1] there may be is paid to the employees, the remainder going to the directors and the ordinary shareholders. Obviously, if a company is paying the highest wages which they regard as prudent, any surplus profits will be much less than if they had been paying the lowest wages at which they could obtain the labour ; and partly as a result of this, and partly because since the initiation of our profit-sharing scheme in 1923, the country has passed through a period of deep trade depression, we have only made distributions of surplus profits on two occasions ; but I believe that the establishment of our profit-sharing scheme has been a thoroughly sound move.

The whole body of employees, through the central council, has elected a profit-sharing committee to whom the financial results of each year's trading are explained in the greatest detail. If there is no distribution, they know, and can pass on their knowledge to the employees generally, that it is because surplus profits have not been earned, and this removes any suspicion that the shareholders are getting away with profits in which the employees might reasonably have been expected to share.

Possibly the darkest cloud hanging over the heads of workers is the fear of unemployment. No system of industry can be regarded as satisfactory which does not reduce that menace to the lowest possible limits. It would be out of place for me, in a book of this kind, to express my views as to what might be done by the State to deal with this problem, though, frankly, I doubt whether it can be dealt with effectively through any other agency.

---

[1] By " surplus profits " is here meant any profits there may be after capital has been remunerated on a scale which, when the profit-sharing scheme was being devised, was regarded as necessary for the financial stability of the business.

We have tried a number of experiments at the Cocoa Works to regularise work so as to avoid the necessity of reducing staff, and also with a view to lessening the hardship which results when dismissals are inevitable. I am sorry to have to admit that we have not succeeded in discovering any novel method of dealing with this extremely difficult problem of unemployment. We have done what every considerate firm does, namely, to try to regularise our sales, which is particularly difficult in a seasonal trade such as ours. Through our employment department we ensure that no man shall be dismissed through slackness in one department if there is suitable work available for him elsewhere in the factory, and we have taken very complete measures to prevent anyone being dismissed for inadequate cause. Where slackness of work in any department is likely to be temporary, it is dealt with by short time, a course warmly supported by the workers themselves. In order to mitigate the hardship caused to those who are dismissed, we have established an unemployment benefit fund to which the company has undertaken to contribute a sum not exceeding one per cent. of the wage bill in any year. This is used to supplement benefits received through the National Unemployment Insurance Fund. The length of time during which such payments are made depends upon the employee's service. We have also been able, in a number of cases, to establish men in small businesses, such as shops, and expert advice has been available to those wishing to enter upon enterprises of this kind. We have experimented without much success in other methods of helping men with whose services we were obliged to dispense. I think it may be said that we have regarded dismissal, especially in times of trade depression, as a very serious matter, and have done our best to avoid dismissing men, and to mitigate the hardship involved where dismissal is inevitable. By all these different means the menace of unemployment has been considerably lessened, but it has not been removed.

Economic insecurity arising through temporary illness is met by the provisions of the National Health Insurance Fund supplemented by sick clubs, to which many workers subscribe. We have dealt with chronic illness through an Invalidity Fund established by the company, and endowed by a gift of 75,000 £1 $7\frac{1}{2}$ per cent. preference shares. This has been of real advantage to a number of employees suffering from long illnesses.

Our Pension Fund provides substantial pensions for workers who remain with us to pension age, but it does not give security to those who leave our service through any cause prior to reaching that age. On leaving the service, such men only receive their own contributions, with $2\frac{1}{2}$ per cent. compound interest. In certain cases where it has been found necessary to part with men who are approaching pension age, arrangements have been made to give them a pension, though less in amount than they would have received had they stayed till sixty-five, the company in that case contributing to the pension fund the lump sum necessary to enable this to be done. A non-contributory scheme of pensions for widows has been greatly appreciated. In connection with the pension fund an arrangement has been entered into whereby if a man dies before reaching pension age, if his own contributions plus $2\frac{1}{2}$ per cent. compound interest do not amount to £100, the deficit is paid by the company. Thus, every member of the pension fund is insured, either through his own payments or by payments made by the company, for £100 should he die before pension age.

A pension fund is an expensive item, but is not

so expensive as would appear if one merely regarded the contributions made to it by the company, because a company having a pension fund giving substantial pensions is justified in fixing a retiring age. In our case, it is sixty-five in the case of men working in the factory, sixty years in that of commercial travellers, and fifty-five in the case of women. Unless substantial pensions were payable, great hardship would be incurred if these retiring ages were insisted upon, and there are many companies who are, on that account, keeping on the pay-roll old employees who are unable to earn their full wages. They are thus paying " hidden " pensions which must often amount to very large sums.

As regards hours of work, we have for nearly twenty years been working a five-day week of forty-four hours in the factory, and thirty-nine hours in the offices. The long week-end is keenly appreciated by the workers, and has undoubtedly had a beneficial effect upon their health.

I pass now from what I may describe as the *basic* welfare conditions in any industrial enterprise— namely, the workers' status, remuneration, economic security, and hours of work, to consider what I may call the *refinements* of welfare work, namely, the provision of well-lit, well-ventilated, and, so far as possible, comfortable workrooms ; the provision of medical services, adequate canteen facilities, and facilities for education and recreation. I have briefly described what we are doing, but I do not think that anything that I have said calls for comment in this chapter, because our activities run very largely on the lines of what is done in many other factories. But I would like to emphasise the importance of this work. Indeed, such welfare work must inevitably be undertaken in any enterprise conducted with due regard to the interests of the community as a whole, for in such an enterprise the employers will naturally seek to establish conditions of work such as they would themselves desire if they were working for others.

Conclusions

I now come to the most difficult part of my task—namely, to assess the significance of the experiments I have just summarised.

As I said in the introduction, the whole of the labour policy at the Cocoa Works has been developed by the directors solely with the purpose of providing good working conditions for the employees, and without any other thought in their minds. But it has become abundantly evident in recent years that there are millions of workers in this country and elsewhere who are dissatisfied with their present conditions, and who are seriously asking whether they would not be better off if the industrial system were changed. In the writing of this book, therefore, I have had in mind the question whether under capitalism it is possible to provide working conditions as good as might reasonably be looked for under any other system of which we have knowledge.

Of course, I am not labouring under the illusion that working conditions at the Cocoa Works represent the best that is being done under the capitalist system, and still less the best that the capitalist system is capable of doing. I am familiar with the labour conditions in a number of factories in different countries, and know how many employers are striving to provide good conditions for their workers. I have only thought it worth while to publish an account of what we are doing for two reasons: first, because some of our experiments are on different lines from those being tried elsewhere; and second, because it is possible that in some matters we are in advance of others, although certainly in many matters others are in advance of us. An exchange of information on questions of this kind is mutually helpful.

I think our experiments do show that it is possible, without lowering efficiency, to accord to the workers a status as good as they would enjoy under any alternative system, and if I am right, then I think this is a matter of real importance, for I am convinced that the workers attach far more importance to the question of their status in industry than is generally supposed. As I pointed out in a preceding chapter,[1] no industry can be efficiently administered by mass meetings, nor indeed by committees. There must be " order givers " and " order takers," and discipline must be maintained. The beliefs at present held by many as to the measure of industrial democracy which would be enjoyed under a socialistic or communistic system would prove, in practice, to be illusory.

With regard to remuneration and working conditions, I am satisfied that it is *possible* under capitalism to provide conditions which compare not unfavourably with those which could be expected under any other system, but it is no satisfaction to the workers to know that a given system of industry is *capable* of providing good conditions unless, in fact, it does so. Taking industrial conditions as a whole, they fall far short of what they might and should be, and it is this fact which is rightly causing discontent among the workers.

Industrial reformers fall into two classes :—

(1) Those who have despaired of remedying present industrial evils save by overthrowing the capitalist system and building up a new one from the foundations, and who are working to bring that about.

[1] See p. 2.

(2) Those who, while very conscious of the present
evils, believe they can best be remedied by evolutionary rather than revolutionary methods, and
are striving to quicken up the process of evolution.

Personally, I believe in evolutionary change. If
we cast our eyes back over the past, we cannot but
be struck by the immense improvement in the lot
of the workers in Great Britain in comparatively
recent times. In this country real wages to-day
are immensely higher than they were twenty-five
years ago.[1] Hours of work, not only for children
but also for adults, are much lower than they were
thirty years ago. Working conditions have immensely
improved, and workers enjoy much greater economic
security through the operation of the Unemployment
Insurance and Health Insurance Acts, the National
Old Age Pension Act, and the Widows' and Orphans'
Pensions Act, all of which have resulted from legislation passed during the last twenty-seven years.
Largely through the influence of the trade unions,
the status of the workers is to-day much higher than
it was, and, moreover, no year passes without recording
still further progress in their lot. In no other country
in the world does the worker enjoy more freedom
than in Britain. He is free to form his own trade
union to look after his interests, and to strike against
his employer if he thinks he is not getting a square
deal. He is free to criticise the Government, and to
organise and agitate to get it changed. No Government can compel him to work in a particular place,
or indeed to work at all. Governments protect him

	Year			Wages	Cost of Living
[1]	1914	.	.	100	100
	1937	.	.	197	147

Extract from table, page 30, in *Wages and Incomes in the United
Kingdom since 1860*, by A. L. Bowley. Cambridge University Press.

against under-payment, but place no upward limits to his earnings.

I cannot but believe that a system which has shown itself capable of such immense improvement during comparatively recent years can, by evolutionary methods, be still further adjusted so that in ever-widening measure industry may come to be conducted in the interests of the community as a whole, and not of a favoured class. But, though it would be a great mistake to ignore the progress which has been and is being made, the fact is that the workers throughout the civilised world have become impatient. Like most of us, they are not so much concerned with comparing existing conditions with those of the past ; they compare them with what they think conditions ought to be. Their impatience has reached a point when the amount of labour unrest is likely to increase, unless the rate of progress in effecting improvements in the workers' lot is speeded up.

Under the present system it rests with those who are in control of industry to say how far they will voluntarily go in seeking to improve the workers' conditions, and how quickly they will move in this direction. I think this is tantamount to saying that it rests with them to determine whether change in the future will come about through evolution or revolution, for change there will undoubtedly be.

APPENDICES

APPENDIX I

AN objection commonly raised to the principle of profit-sharing is that statistics show that a large proportion of profit-sharing schemes have been abandoned.

The first step taken in our investigation was to analyse the statements of the employers concerned in the abandoned schemes. The average reader sees from a newspaper summary of a Government report that fifty-five per cent. of the profit-sharing schemes commenced have been discontinued after an average duration of eight years. He does not realise that the fact that a scheme is abandoned is no proof of its having been a failure. Schemes abandoned include those given up for all causes, including, for example, the death of the employer after many years' successful experience of profit-sharing. The percentage of failures is not, therefore, as great as the percentage of abandoned schemes.

Furthermore, even where schemes have been failures, this may be due not so much to a defect in the theory behind profit-sharing, as to some defect in the particular scheme, or some departure from the true principles of profit-sharing, or to some extraneous conditions or events. Our examination showed that the employers concerned only wrote down thirty-six per cent. of the abandoned schemes as failures. Next, an analysis was made of all the available opinions of employers as to the degree of success achieved by their schemes, whether abandoned or continuing, with the following result :—

Thorough or substantial success	. .	66 per cent.
Fair, but on the whole disappointing	.	14 ,,
Failures	.	20 ,,

Finally, each case was taken in detail, consideration being given not only to the fact and cause of abandonment (where the scheme had been abandoned) and to the employer's opinion, but also to all other relevant information. In 230 cases sufficient information was available for an analysis to be made, with the following result :—

Successes . . . . . . 63 per cent.
Failures . . . . . . 37 ,,

An analysis was then made of the eighty-four cases written down as failures. In twenty of these the information was insufficient to justify any definite conclusion as to the precise cause of failure ; in seventeen cases the scheme had failed to serve as a method of payment by results (which, of course, is what one would anticipate) ; in nine cases the scheme had failed to constitute a successful weapon against trade unionism, and had therefore been dropped ; and in nine cases there were serious and obvious defects in the schemes themselves. In eight cases, chiefly agricultural, there was no real possibility of profit from the outset. In a considerable proportion of the remaining cases there were special or qualifying circumstances. To quote any precise figure as to the true failures might be misleading. However, the investigation showed that the chances of success for a profit-sharing scheme, properly devised and administered, were much greater than is currently believed, and that indeed such a scheme, assuming time to become established, might be expected to be advantageous to all parties concerned.

If this be so, what is the real contribution of profit-sharing ? Its success appears to consist primarily in the creation of better relations between employer and employed. We have been mistaken in regarding it simply from the standpoint of financial inducement ; it should be regarded rather from the psychological point of view. In other words, its results have depended not primarily on how much employees have actually received, but rather on their knowledge that *whatever profits resulted* from the joint efforts of all concerned would be divided amongst them on some basis previously agreed upon as equitable.

Profit-sharing tends to satisfy two fundamental aspirations of labour. The first is the average man's desire for adventure. I have often stressed, and stress again in this book, the worker's desire for security, and I believe this to be a very real and important desire. However, security alone will not provide a completely satisfying outlook for life. Man is an adventurous animal, and he must find some outlet for his adventurous instincts. There is little of adventure in the industrial outlook of the average trade unionist who reaches full scale round about twenty-one years of age, and, at the best, sees little prospect of any increase in the return for his efforts for the rest of his working life. A profit-sharing scheme may, to some extent, restore to him that interest in the results of his endeavours which he would formerly have had as a craftsman working on his own account. It links him up with a joint adventure.

The second need which profit-sharing tends to satisfy is the almost universal aspiration after justice. The worker wants to have a " square deal." He is prepared to share in the misfortunes of his employer if he is satisfied that these misfortunes are real and that when better days come he will share in the good fortune. The wage system does not constitute a very definite and obvious guarantee in this direction, although in the long run, in economic theory, it may broadly have this effect. The second contribution which profit-sharing makes, therefore, is in informing the worker as to what the position of his business is year by year with regard to profits, and in giving him a guarantee that if and when there are surplus profits he will get his share.

An objection often made to profit-sharing is that it will fail eventually, when profits fail, because the workers will not be sufficiently educated to understand the fundamental economics of the situation. This may be so, but the obvious moral is that an effort should be made to *make* them understand the simple fundamentals underlying industry. If so, the existence of a profit-sharing scheme constitutes an invaluable opportunity to " put over " this education. This educational effort, and this granting to employees of a wider knowledge of the general operations of the business in which they are employed, are desirable things in themselves which should be attempted in any case, and profit-sharing facilitates the attempt.

Other objections to profit-sharing come from both employers and organised labour. One objection is that an employer cannot afford to give that publicity to his affairs which profit-sharing demands. This may be so in the case of small employers, but I do not think it is an objection in the case of a joint stock company. A further objection raised is that profit-sharing makes it harder for the less profitable business in an industry to compete with the more successful. In other words, it "breaks down the solidarity" of employers! But even in so far as this is true, it is only an acceleration of a process which is continually going on, and which the economists claim as one of the outstanding merits of the present system. A similar objection arises as between one industry and another, and here it is more serious, because it does not follow, as in the former case, that one industry is for the moment less profitable than another because it is less efficient. However, it seems to me that this difficulty is over-stressed. Those who put it forward are apt to exaggerate the mobility of labour. Another objection made to profit-sharing is that it penalises the home investor. But this seems to overlook the fact that the return on capital is largely determined by the risk, and that if, as we assume, profit-sharing makes for increased efficiency and therefore leads to greater security, the investor should be prepared to receive a correspondingly lower return. A well-founded objection is that labour may receive a share of surplus profits for which in a particular instance the commercial side of the business may be wholly responsible, or may, through a mistake in a firm's commercial policy, or by some untoward circumstance, be deprived of any reward for a year's increased effort. This is, however, a difficulty inherent in any partnership. A final objection is, that if labour is to share in profits it must also agree to bear its proportion of losses. Whatever be the truth in this, it may be pointed out, first, that if labour, as a result of a profit-sharing scheme, gives for a whole year better service than it would otherwise have done, and at

N

the end receives no share of profits, it is, in a very true sense, actually bearing its share of losses, since it is not recouped for its additional effort. Secondly, under an ordinary scheme, labour shares only in the *surplus* profits—*i.e.* any profits there may be after necessary reserves have been set aside and after shareholders have received whatever interest may be necessary to render investment in the company's shares sufficiently attractive to enable further capital to be raised, on reasonable terms, should occasion arise. This rate of interest will necessarily include, first, payment for the loan of capital at the rate payable for capital which is adequately secured, and, second, an insurance premium sufficient to cover the risk run. If capital's wage (which covers the payment for risk) is cumulative, then the workers are, in effect, sharing in losses.

The real objection and the greatest difficulty are found in the attitude of organised labour. I cannot refer in more than the briefest terms to this matter, and would merely say that labour generally is not prepared willingly to accept any profit-sharing scheme which does not satisfy the following detailed conditions, namely, that—

(1) the amount of capital which is adopted as the basis of the scheme really represents assets ; that is to say, that capital has not been inflated ;

(2) labour's proportion of profits is fixed, and the share it will receive cannot be reduced by any manipulation of reserves, or by unreasonable increases in rewards of management, or similar methods ;

(3) labour has adequate means of satisfying itself as to the accuracy of the accounts ;

(4) labour has a legal right to its share, and is not dependent upon the bounty of employers ;

(5) there are no unreasonable provisions restricting the mobility or freedom of labour;

(6) wages are not to be less than trade union or other appropriate rates ;

(7) employees are to be free to join any trade union ; and

(8) strikes are not to be penalised.

Further, organised labour as a rule feels that even if these conditions are satisfied, profit-sharing, as usually understood, may tend to weaken trade union solidarity. In this I think it is right. Nevertheless, profit-sharing schemes can be devised which, in various ways, will meet this objection.

The advanced labour man's point of view is quite different from that of the orthodox trade unionist. His claim is that any sharing of profits will tend to perpetuate the profit-making system. He will generally admit, however, that, under any system he contemplates, something in the nature of profits would have to be shared between producers and the community, and that a good profit-sharing scheme might conceivably point the way to further developments. His real fear, of course, is that labour will be made content.

I cannot here deal with the relative merits of profit-sharing and co-partnership. As I understand it, the latter consists of a share of (1) profits, (2) control, and (3) capital. The first I have just discussed. The second is discussed in Chapter I. The third is a question to be considered by the employer and by the trade unions, in relation to the particular circumstances of the business and the industry.

To sum up, I feel that the factory is likely to be a more efficient working unit if the workers are given some direct financial interest, not only in the performance of their individual jobs, but in the success of the whole undertaking.

APPENDIX II

Friendly Societies

The male employees at the Cocoa Works have for many years run a Friendly Society on their own account. Beyond supplementing the small death benefit by the society, the company makes no money grants, but undertakes to collect the subscriptions for members. This is done by deducting the amount of the subscription from the wages, with the authority of the member, and handing the sum thus collected to the secretary of the society. This not only saves the society considerable trouble and expense, but undoubtedly encourages many employees to remain in the society, whose membership would lapse were not their subscriptions thus automatically collected without effort on their part.

The society has been in existence since 1910, and took the place of an old Dividing or Slate Club, which had been run for about twenty years. At the end of 1937 there were about 900 members. The weekly contributions vary, but members may pay up to 6d. per week, which entitles them to sickness benefit at the rate of 12s. per week for twenty-six weeks. The society records are examined periodically by an actuary, and its financial policy is based on his advice.

The women employees have not deemed it advisable to form a Friendly Society, but have established a successful Sick Club that has nearly 2,000 members and an adequate reserve. The contribution paid is 2d. per week, and any girl in the regular employ of the company is eligible to join after a minimum of three months' employment. The club is governed by a committee of seven members. The benefit is payable after six months' membership of the club, and is at the rate of 7s. per week for those who have been members for four years, and 5s. a week for those with a shorter term of membership. Payment is continued at the full rate for the first six weeks of illness, and at half rate for a subsequent six weeks. Members who are ill less than four days are not entitled to any benefit. During the year 1937 a total of £679 was paid out to 865 members of the Girls' Sick Club.

In the largest of the girls' departments further benefits are provided from a subscription of 2d. a week from seniors and 1d. from juniors. This subscription entitles senior subscribers to a single payment of 10s. after twelve weeks' absence due to sickness, and, at further intervals of twelve weeks, to payments of 8s., 6s., and finally 4s. Junior subscribers are entitled to half these benefits.

In addition to the above, in ten of the men's and four of the girls' departments small " shop clubs " have been started. These were formed during the war, when, owing to the high cost of living, employees wished to augment the amount of benefit received during sickness. At the end of each year in most of the clubs, the sum of money remaining after paying expenses and benefits, and carrying a certain amount forward, is shared among the members. These " clubs " have taken the place of *ad hoc* collections taken up by his workmates when an employee was sick. They equalise the benefits which formerly used to vary with, or even depend upon, the popularity of the individual.

APPENDIX III

Roast Beef and Yorkshire Pudding . .	8d. and 6d.
Hot Pot and Peas	6d.
Fish Cake and Chips	3d.
Fish and Chips	3d.
Sausages and Potatoes	2½d.
Savoury and Potatoes	2½d.
Sausage Patties	2½d.
Soup	2d.
Apple Pudding	2d.
Rice Pudding	2d.
Chipped Potatoes	1d.
Mashed Potatoes and Gravy . . .	1d.
Cakes (various)	1d.
Tea (per cup)	1d.
Cocoa (per cup)	1d.
Lime Juice	1d.

Restaurant

Soup.	Green Pea	4d.
Fish.	Fried Plaice and Anchovy Sauce	10d.
Meats.	Roast Stuffed Shoulder of Mutton	1s.
	Mock Grill	10d.
	Rissole	8d.
	Cold Tongue	1s.
Vegetarian.	Egg au Gratin	8d.
Vegetables.	Mashed Potatoes . . .	3d.
	Potato Balls	3d.
	Buttered Carrots . . .	3d.

Puddings.	Fruit Salad and Cream	. .	6d.
	Ginger Sponge Pudding	. .	6d.
	Banana and Apricot Tartlet	.	6d.
	Vermicelli Pudding	. . .	6d.
	Tea and Coffee	. . .	2d. and 3d.

A luncheon, consisting of soup or coffee, fish or entrée, vegetables, and sweet or cheese and biscuits, costs 1s. 6d.

APPENDIX IV

LIST OF RECREATIONAL ACTIVITIES

Association football : 24 departmental teams, 16 shift (youths' teams), 6 teams playing " friendly " games, 2 teams playing league games.

Rugby football : 3 teams.

Hockey : 2 men's teams ; 3 women's teams.

Cricket : 2 men's teams ; 1 women's team ; and 220 playing informal cricket.

Netball : 2 girls' teams.

Baseball : 12 youths' teams.

Swimming Club : 1 mixed and 1 for women only.

Tennis : Mixed membership. There is also a junior tennis club where girls are coached.

Rounders : 2 girls' teams.

Boys' Club : Billiards, Darts, Table Tennis, Boxing, Cycling.

Youths' Club : Harriers, Camping, Discussion Groups, etc.

Rowing.

Badminton (mixed).

Weight-lifting.

Allotments for men (see p. 138).

Girl Guides.

St. John's Ambulance Division and V.A.D., First Aid and Home Nursing (women).

First Aid Classes (men).

Rowntree Prize Band.

Orchestral Society (mixed).

Choral Society (mixed).

Operatic Society.

The Rowntree Players (mixed).

The Actors' Club (youths and girls under 21).

The Rowntree Concert Party (girls). Membership, 20.

Nativity Play.

Handwork Classes (mixed) : Art Metal Work, Woodwork and Joinery, Sketching Club, Embroidery, Dressmaking, etc. (An Arts and Crafts Exhibition of hobbies undertaken either at home or in connection with Works Societies is held annually.)

Photographic Society.

Moor and Fell Club.

Rambling Club.

Magazine Club.

Keep Fit, for men and youths.

Physical Training for women and girls, including " Keep Fit," Greek, Country, National, Ballroom (mixed) and Tap Dancing, and Gymnastics.

APPENDIX V

SECTION A

EMPLOYMENT

1. Each employee is required to pass the Works Doctor before commencing work with the company, unless in the particular instance it is not practicable, in which case the employee must do so before completing fourteen days' service. Seasonal, temporary, and casual workers undergo a restricted medical examination, but must pass the full medical test before being taken on to the ordinary staff.

Members of the Building Contract Staff are not required to submit themselves to the doctor until they have been employed continuously for nine months.

2. No employee may be dismissed until his or her case has been referred by the management (in the case of girls after discussion with the personnel assistant) to the Employment Department, including the chief shop steward.

When it is proposed to dismiss employees on account of lack of work, the list of those selected for dismissal shall be submitted to the shop steward, before the notices are issued, for his or her information and approval. In the event of non-agreement, each case will be further considered by the management and shop steward in conjunction with the Employment Department with whom the final decision rests. In all other cases of dismissal the shop steward will be informed of the reasons for dismissal before notice is issued.

3. Any employee convicted of a criminal offence or guilty of immorality or other misconduct will be

202

dealt with by the management by dismissal or otherwise (subject to the right of appeal under Rule 70) on the principles in operation on 1st December 1922, with such variations as are from time to time determined by the directors with the approval of the executive committee of the central works council. If such circumstance occurred before, and was not disclosed upon, engagement, the employee will be similarly dealt with.

Note. A summary of the principles referred to and of variations thereof is maintained by the management and is furnished from time to time to the chief shop steward and the personnel assistants.

4. Married women may be employed only in exceptional circumstances, such as for seasonal trade and the like. Female employees, therefore, on marriage, will relinquish their employment with the company.

5. The maximum age at which employees shall retire is sixty-five in the case of men, and fifty-five in the case of women, at which ages, respectively, subscribers to the company's Pension Fund become entitled to pensions, and members of the Auxiliary Retirement Fund become entitled to their benefits.

6. No particular job can be guaranteed to any worker. The management has the right to transfer an employee at its discretion when the distribution of work in the factory makes this necessary. When it is proposed to transfer factory employees, the list of those selected for transfer must be shown to the shop steward or shop stewards concerned for information before the transfers are made.

7. From time to time unforeseen circumstances occur which necessitate the immediate placing of employees on short time without the notice prescribed by the company's Standing Orders and Instructions. Previous intimation will, however, be given at the earliest practicable moment. When employees are placed on short time without the prescribed notice, immediate intimation thereof must be given to the labour manager.

SECTION B

WAGES

8. Subject as herein provided, wages fixed by the day or week are payable for a full working week, and in the event of an employee working less than a full week a proportionate part of such wage is payable.

9. GUARANTEE AS TO PIECE AND BONUS RATES.

Existing rates (standard of output) will not be altered unless it is agreed with the workers' representatives that a change affecting the rate of output attainable for the same effort has taken place in—

(*a*) machine or other equipment,
(*b*) material used,
(*c*) process or method of manufacture, or
(*d*) other conditions.

Wherever it is agreed that a mistake has been made in the setting of a rate, correction will be made without delay.

Subject to what has been said above, the company *guarantee that the standard output required to earn standard piece or bonus money will remain unaltered except as provided above, and that standard outputs on new jobs (including all existing jobs for which the final rate has not yet been set) will be similarly guaranteed when sufficient time and practice have been allowed for attaining normal skill on the job.*

Note. Standard piece is ascertained in accordance with Clause VII of the Industrial Agreement, as modified in accordance with the company's special arrangement with the workers' representatives. It is subject to alteration by the I.I.R.C. or by agreement with the workers' representatives, and this guarantee does not preclude any such alteration.

Piece Rates.

10. When the management, for the purpose of fixing a piece rate, employs time study to determine the standard method or the standard output, the employees to be

studied will be selected by the management and approved by the shop steward. Before being put into operation the standard output will be submitted to the shop steward concerned for his comments and approval.

11. In the case of new work, the piece rate will be regarded as temporary until normal skill and speed are acquired, when a permanent rate will be fixed. In all cases rates of pay must be announced to workers before they begin on any job.

12. INTERRUPTIONS TO PRODUCTION.

(a) Where interruptions or delays to production are due to hot weather, or to temporary defects in or breakdowns of machinery over which the workers have no control, provided that the time is more than one hour per day, and that the workers in question are sent off work, payment will be made as provided in Clause III of the Industrial Agreement.

No payment will be made where reasonable alternative work has been offered and refused. Where such alternative work is provided, payment will be at prevailing rates.

(b) Whenever—
    (1) there is a deficiency in the supply of materials, or
    (2) the supply of materials has failed, or
    (3) the materials are not of normal quality, or
    (4) the machines are working unsatisfactorily with the result that the output of piece-workers is stopped or restricted, payment will be made at the rate of average earnings for the time so lost.

Workers are required to notify overlookers directly or through the shop stewards immediately the fact of such deficiency or failure, or of unsatisfactory materials, or of unsatisfactory working of machines becomes evident.

13. PAYMENT FOR OVERTIME.

(a) Except in the case of shift workers, or workers to whom special arrangements with regard to the working week apply, or those whose whole working times are governed by trade union rules, all workers (men and women) whether day workers or piece-workers will be paid for overtime in accordance with the following arrangements :—

Days of the Week.	Rate of Overtime Payment.
On Mondays, Tuesdays, Wednesdays, and Thursdays after nine and a half hours have been worked. On Fridays after nine hours have been worked. On Saturdays whatever time is worked (whether foreseen or unforeseen).	Time and a quarter for the first two hours, and time and a half after the first two hours.
From Saturday midnight until 6 a.m. Monday.	Double time.

Note 1. Each day stands by itself.

Note 2. Employees who work on Saturday morning as part of their arranged week will not receive overtime pay for the Saturday morning unless they have worked forty-seven hours at ordinary rates during the working week.

(*b*) Employees engaged on shifts receive overtime pay at the above overtime rates after the arranged shift has been completed, with the exception that all time worked on Saturdays or during the week-end will be paid for as follows :—

(1) After forty-four hours have been worked during the current week, time and a quarter for the first two hours, and time and a half afterwards.

(2) Between 12 noon and the following midnight, time and a half.

(3) Between Saturday midnight and Sunday midnight, double time.

Note 1. Each shift stands by itself.

Note 2. In addition to the above payments a proportionate amount of shift bonus will be added, based on hours actually worked.

(*c*) Employees engaged on mutually arranged night turns of work will receive overtime pay after forty-seven hours have been worked during the working week. Such overtime will be paid for as follows :—

Time and a quarter for the first two hours on any occasion, and time and a half afterwards.

Note 1. In addition to the above payments a proportionate amount of night bonus will be added, based on hours actually worked.

(*d*) Time worked on a Bank Holiday will be paid at the appropriate overtime rates only after a period has been worked equal to eight and a half hours when the holiday falls on a Monday or Friday, or nine hours when it falls on any other day of the week.

14. Payment for Work during Annual or Bank Holidays.

(*a*) Employees who are called in during the annual holiday on the understanding that they will take a vacation at a date agreeable to the management, and are engaged on cleaning or on work other than their ordinary work, or on their ordinary work under abnormal conditions, will be paid as follows :—

Piece and bonus workers : average weekly earnings.
Day workers : ordinary day rates.

Note 1. Such workers will be paid at the rates specified in Rule 44 (*c*) for the period which they take as a vacation.

Note 2. Average rate of earnings in respect of work done during holiday week includes any sum or payment for merit, for taking charge, or for night or shift bonus.

(*b*) Whenever workers who are not entitled to any holiday allowance are found work during holiday week at their own request, they will be paid the prevailing rates of pay for the job.

(*c*) Employees who are called in on any Bank Holiday will be paid at the rates specified in paragraph (*a*), plus the holiday allowance for that day.

Note. Average rate of earnings in respect of work done on Bank Holidays includes any sum or payment for merit, for taking charge, or for night or shift bonus.

15. PAYMENT FOR WORK DURING STOCKTAKING.

When engaged in cleaning, etc., during stocktaking, piece-workers will be paid the standard day rate (according to age) as fixed by the Industrial Agreement. Where any piece-worker normally receives in addition to the normal piece day wage and piece rate a sum or payment for some special qualification or merit, such additional sum will be added to the standard day rate payable under this paragraph.

Day and bonus workers will receive their ordinary standard day rate even though such rate is above the minimum for their ages as fixed by the Industrial Agreement.

16. TRANSFERS.

(*a*) Workers transferred for short periods from their ordinary occupation, on grounds other than shortage of work, to work on which a learning period is not deemed advisable, will in general be paid not less than their average earnings at their ordinary occupation. Where such transfer is to piece or bonus work for which a learning period is deemed necessary, the length of learning period will be agreed and an allowance given, expressed as an addition to the piece earnings. This will be so fixed as to lift the return for equivalent effort to the average rate of earnings of the group or individual transferred. The management will set and revise this allowance in consultation with the appropriate shop steward, having regard to the rate at which the new work can be learnt.

(*b*) Where transfers result from shortage of work, workers transferred in consequence will take the rates of pay prevailing in the section to which they have been transferred.

(*c*) Where the circumstances attending transfers are exceptional, the management, after consultation with the appropriate shop steward, will fix the rate of remuneration according to the merit of the case and the type of work.

17. Shift Work.

Normal shift work performed between Saturday midnight and Sunday midnight will be paid at double-time rates.

When a period of shift work is about to conclude, reasonable notice will be posted in the department concerned ; if such notice is posted later than the termination of the Thursday shift of any particular employee, such employee will be paid the extra allowance for shift workers for the week following the conclusion of the period, except where, in consequence of the conclusion of a shift, the men are transferred to night work. A shift will not be terminated merely on account of a holiday interruption.

18. Payment to Employees attending Meetings or on Deputations.

Where employees, after clocking in, are drawn from their work to attend meetings of the works councils or committees, or to see the manager, or to attend as members of a deputation to a director, departmental manager, or others authorised to receive deputations, and return to their work immediately the meeting or interview is concluded, they will be paid for the time so spent at their average wage in the case of piece or bonus workers, and at their usual rate in the case of day workers. Employees attending at a meeting or on a deputation outside their own department should inform their overlooker or other authorised person before leaving the department.

19. Payment to Workers' Representatives attending Council Meetings or Committees after Factory Hours.

Where councils or committees officially summoned to meet during working hours are continued after leaving time, no payment will be made unless the meeting continues for more than half an hour after ordinary working hours, in which case members (other than those on salary) will be paid for the whole time spent beyond working hours at the ordinary rate, as distinct from overtime rate.

Shift or night workers coming to the works solely for the purpose of attending such councils or committees

o

will receive payment at ordinary rates for the time actually spent in the meeting, but not for " walking time." Where the meeting lasts for less than an hour, a full hour's payment will be made.

20. TIME SPENT AT COUNCILS AND COMMITTEES.

The minutes of each council and committee meeting attended by workers' representatives shall contain a statement as to the time when the meeting began and ended. Should any question arise as to the time spent at a meeting, either the workers' representatives or the overlooker concerned may call for the minutes. The fact that some employees have to make a change of costume will be taken into account.

21. MEDICAL—PAYMENTS.

(a) Employees visiting the doctor, dentist, or optician, and any who, by reason of illness or other sufficient cause are detained in a rest room, will receive payment for the time so spent at I.I.R.C. minimum day rates in the case of piece-workers and at ordinary rates in the case of day workers.

(b) Employees sent home by the doctor, or going home with the doctor's permission, after an accident at the works will receive payment at the rate of their average earnings for the time lost on the day on which they are sent home.

22. " SNACK " TIME.

Except where otherwise arranged, " snack " time will be allowed (with no deduction) as follows :—

    (a) Men working on either of the shifts between 6 a.m. and 10 p.m. :
        Twenty minutes " snack " time each shift.

    (b) Men working at night :
        " Snack " intervals not to exceed a total of twenty minutes each shift, except in the case of men working overtime, when an allowance of a further ten minutes will be made.

Arrangements for the allocation of these intervals shall follow the choice of the workers, except where the efficient working of machinery or plant may make it necessary for the management to formulate the original proposals, or to require other arrangements.

23. LUNCH IN WORK-ROOMS.

All female employees will be allowed a ten minutes' break for lunch each morning, conditional upon their remaining at their places and turning away from the work-tables. Tea or cocoa will be supplied to those wishing to purchase it. Any not wishing to take lunch will be at liberty to continue their work.

Female employees working until six o'clock on any afternoon, or when engaged in cleaning during the general stocktaking period, will similarly be allowed a ten minutes' break in the afternoon, during which they may purchase tea or cocoa.

Female office staff will be allowed a ten minutes' break each morning if commencing work at 8.30 a.m. or earlier, and a similar break each afternoon when working a minimum of four and a half hours.

SECTION C

APPOINTMENTS AND PROMOTIONS

24. FILLING OF VACANCIES.

(a) All vacancies in office departments will be advertised on the company's notice-boards unless it has been previously agreed with the chief clerical shop steward that such advertisement is not necessary.

(b) When there is a definite vacancy in an administrative post in a factory department, no employee will be transferred from another department to fill such vacancy if there is in the former department a person who, in the opinion of the director or manager concerned, has equal qualifications for taking up the post.

(c) The manager of the department concerned will consult with the workers through the shop steward before an overlooker is appointed, or promoted to a higher grade of the overlooking staff, and in the latter case with a representative of the overlookers from whom it is proposed to make the promotion.

(*d*) All non-administrative vacancies will be advertised in the department concerned, unless the appropriate shop steward is of opinion that in any particular case this is unnecessary ; and in filling them the management will take into account length of service along with the other necessary qualifications for the post. When a position is likely to be temporary a notice to that effect will be appended to the notice of the vacancy.

(*e*) Before an appointment to a non-administrative post which has been advertised is made, the shop steward will be consulted.

(*f*) Before offering piece-work to employees transferred from one department to another, due regard will be paid to the claims to piece-work of day workers already working in the latter department.

SECTION D

DISCIPLINE

25. STARTING AND FINISHING WORK WHEN BELL RINGS.

Employees must start work promptly when the bell rings, but not before, and they must not cease work until the time officially fixed for their department.

26. ARTICLES NOT ALLOWED IN WORKROOMS.

Workers are not allowed to take into the workrooms dinner baskets, bags, or similar receptacles, pins, needles, face powder, lipsticks, or any personal article made of glass, or anything else which the management considers might get into the goods.

Note. This rule does not apply to paper parcels containing lunch and nothing else.

27. TAKING OF CHOCOLATE, ETC.

The taking of chocolate, sweets, or ingredients, the property of the company, whether with a view to eating them on the premises or otherwise disposing of them, is not allowed. Nor should they be handed to visitors or guides touring the works.

28. CLEANLINESS.

In the interest of health and cleanliness :

(*a*) All employees must wash their hands thoroughly before handling foodstuffs, especially before returning to their work after visiting the lavatory.

(*b*) Spitting on the company's premises is forbidden.

(*c*) Snuff-taking and the chewing of tobacco and chewing-gum in workrooms are forbidden.

29. SMOKING.

Smoking is strictly forbidden in all parts of the works, offices, warehouses, yards, lavatories, or premises, except in the dining-rooms, smoke-rooms, and certain other rooms expressly approved by the chairman of the York Board. This rule may, in the case of builders engaged on new outside construction, be waived by agreement between the building department manager and the head of the fire brigade.

30. AUTOMATIC FIRE ALARM.

Employees must not interfere with any of the instruments or wires connected with the Automatic Fire Alarm System. Any accidental interference with any part of the installation must be reported at once to the overlooker, who must promptly inform the head of the fire brigade.

31. CARE OF PROPERTY.

Employees must take every possible care of machinery, materials, ingredients, and other property of the company, and must exercise the utmost care to avoid waste in doing their work, and to prevent any form of contamination.

32. CAPS AND OVERALLS.

The wearing of caps of standard pattern and suitable texture and overalls to match is compulsory for all women operatives who check in on factory clocks, and for women overlookers. Each such employee must provide herself with cap and overall on entering the company's service, keep them repaired and cleaned, and renew them at her own expense when necessary.

33. MATCHES, ETC.

Tapers or patent gas lighters only must be used for lighting gas, etc., and safety matches for lighting tapers. Matches must be carefully extinguished to avoid risk of fire, and must not be thrown on the floor.

34. BICYCLES.

Bicycles must not at any time be ridden up or down the Time Office Avenues or the road on the north side of the gum department fruit rooms.

Bicycles must not be ridden within the company's premises at the factory or office leaving times nor within five minutes after such times, except when and where special permission has been obtained.

Bicycles ridden within the company's premises must be ridden with caution and with due regard for other traffic.

No persons other than the owner shall take any bicycle or part of a bicycle from the bicycle sheds without having either the consent of the owner or other sufficient authority.

35. BLOCKING OF GUTTERS AND DRAINS.

Paper and other material must not be thrown out of the factory windows ; the practice, besides leading to untidiness, would cause gutters and drains to become blocked, and might result in serious damage.

36. BETTING AND GAMBLING.

Betting, taking part in raffles or sweepstakes, and the playing of any game of chance for money on any part of the company's premises are prohibited.

37. SALES INSIDE THE FACTORY.

The sale, in the works or offices, of watches, jewellery, photographs, Christmas cards, etc., is not allowed.

38. RESPONSIBILITY FOR PERSONAL PROPERTY.

The company does not hold itself responsible for the personal property of employees, though it takes reasonable precautions to safeguard it.

39. Riding on Vehicles.

No person is allowed to ride upon or in any vehicle belonging to or employed in the service of the company whilst the same is being used for the company's purposes, except the following persons, whilst in the discharge of their duties :—

(*a*) Duly appointed drivers.

(*b*) Members of the transport staff.

(*c*) Mechanics engaged on the repair or testing of the vehicle.

(*d*) Persons actually engaged in loading or unloading the vehicle.

(*e*) Persons having special authority so to do.

40. Emergency Exit Doors.

Emergency exit doors must not be used except in cases of fire or other emergency.

41. Entering and leaving Departments.

Employees must not, without proper permission, enter departments into which their regular work does not take them. Employees leaving workrooms at the end of a working period should do so in a quiet and orderly manner, and good order must be maintained after leaving the factory premises.

42. Change of Address.

Employees changing their address must at once notify their overlooker or, in the case of the salaried staff, the staff office.

43. Employees committing any—

(*a*) breach of the Works Rules,

(*b*) misconduct in their capacity of employees or affecting them as employees, or

(*c*) theft

are liable to dismissal, suspension, or other disciplinary action.

SECTION E

HOLIDAYS

44. ANNUAL HOLIDAY.

(*a*) In addition to the statutory holidays provided for in the Factory Acts, an annual holiday with pay is given to each worker who has been in the continuous employment of the company for a period of not less than six months. The length of a holiday will be proportioned to service as follows (the period of service being counted from 31st July, or in the case of the building department, 30th April in each year) :—

Period of Continuous Service.			Holiday Allowance.
6 months and under 7	. . . .	$2\frac{1}{2}$ days
7 „ „ 8	. . . .	3 „
8 „ „ 9	. . . .	$3\frac{1}{2}$ „
9 „ „ 10	. . . .	4 „
10 „ „ 11	. . . .	$4\frac{1}{2}$ „
11 „ and over	. . . .	5 „

Note. Employees leaving between one holiday and the next will receive a proportion of holiday payment based on the above scale, and on their period of continuous service not taken into account at the previous holiday. This payment is not made to employees who have left without giving proper notice or who have been dismissed for misconduct or incompetence.

(*b*) All workers are required to take a holiday for the period for which holiday pay is due to them under the terms of paragraph (*a*) above.

(*c*) In respect of holidays, piece and bonus workers receive I.I.R.C. minimum day rates and day workers their ordinary day rates.

45. BANK HOLIDAYS.

(*a*) Payment will be made each year for four Bank Holidays and for Christmas Day and Good Friday, and will be allowed to all employees on the company's books

on the holiday in question and also to employees who
leave on the last preceding working day before such
holiday or within forty-eight hours before such last
working day and have been in the service of the company
for at least six months immediately preceding their
leaving.

(b) In respect of holidays, piece and bonus workers
receive I.I.R.C. minimum day rates and day workers
their ordinary day rates.

46. HOLIDAY PAY FOR ABSENTEES.

(a) Holiday payment on the above conditions will be
made to employees who are on the company's books at
the date of the holiday week, or when a Bank Holiday
for which payment is due under the Industrial Agreement
comes round, but who are absent through illness or with
leave, provided that the absence or leave has not exceeded
the twelve months immediately preceding the holiday.

(b) Where an employee is receiving compensation under
the Workmen's Compensation Act, the compensation in
respect of the period covered by the holiday will be made
up to the amount of the holiday pay.

(c) Where an employee in receipt of a grant from the
Invalidity Fund is working part time for the company,
his holiday pay will be in proportion to the time he is
working ; otherwise employees in receipt of a grant from
the Invalidity Fund are not entitled to holiday pay.

47. ARRANGEMENT OF HOURS FOR SHIFT WORKERS AT THE ANNUAL OR BANK HOLIDAYS.

Managers will, prior to each holiday, review this matter
along with the workers concerned and come to an arrangement by mutual agreement whereby, before or after the
holiday, the full working week, allowing for the holiday
hours, may be made up. The arrangement which suits
the majority of the workers will be adopted, provided the
scheme is a workable one from the managerial point of
view.

SECTION F

LEAVE OF ABSENCE

48. GENERAL.

Leave of absence for adequate reasons is obtainable on request from the management, when the granting of leave will not interfere with the satisfactory and economical working of sections of departments. Individual leave will be given by a written permit which must be left by the employee with the gatekeeper at the exit or at the time office.

49. LEAVE FOR A SECTION OF WORKERS.

Leave for a section of workers or requests for alteration of hours to enable a section of workers to attend athletic or other gatherings will be granted only after approval by the manager of the division to which the section belongs.

50. LEAVE FOR YORK RACES.

In departments where conditions of work will allow, leave of absence will be granted, both to male and female employees, for one afternoon selected by the management, but no leave of absence can be granted for any of the other race days. Application must be made not less than three clear days before the afternoon selected.

Note. The central works council desires to point out that absence of employees at the races or other gatherings may necessitate the compulsory closing down of whole departments, affecting many workers, and that employees should consider this responsibility before asking for leave.

51. LEAVE FOR EXTENDED HOLIDAY.

When workers desire an extension of their holiday either before or after the agreed holiday week or on Bank Holidays or at other times, endeavours will be made to meet them as far as the needs of production permit, provided that in all but exceptional cases not less than three weeks' notice is given in respect of an extension of the holiday week, and not less than one week's notice in respect of the extension of Bank Holiday leave.

52. LEAVE FOR MARRIAGE.

Men with not less than seven years' continuous service are, on the occasion of their marriage, granted three days' special leave of absence with full pay.

53. ABSENTEES.

(a) Factory employees who are unable to come to work should at once send a written explanation to the manager.

(b) Except in cases of illness or other serious emergency, factory employees may not absent themselves from work without having previously obtained an official permit. These permits must be left at the time office or with the gatekeeper at the exit.

(c) Clerical employees should report their absence without delay to the head of their department; where absence owing to sickness exceeds three days, a doctor's certificate should be obtained and sent to the staff office.

SECTION G

TIME-KEEPING

54. CLOCKING.

(a) Employees must clock in at the commencement of each working period at the clock provided for their department.

(b) Shift workers and detached staffs such as stablemen, etc., must clock both in and out, unless instructions to the contrary are in any special case issued by the management.

(c) For men engaged on night work the management fix a supper time which applies to the whole of a section or department. When going to supper at this time men will not clock out; if on any occasion they go at any other time, they must clock both in and out. Should overtime lead to a change in supper time for a section, it is necessary to clock both in and out. On returning from supper men must always clock in.

(*d*) Other employees leaving at ordinary factory hours need not clock out, but—

(1) Employees leaving at times other than ordinary factory hours must clock out.

(2) Employees going to and returning from classes need not clock, but must produce to the time office the prescribed attendance card on leaving, collect it on returning, and use only the exits named on it.

(*e*) Employees who are called out at night, or who arrive to carry out an emergency job when the card racks are locked, or whose cards are not immediately available, should obtain an " emergency " card and stamp it " in " or " out " at the central time office entrance, returning the card to the attendant.

55. TIME ALLOWANCE.

There is a universal time allowance throughout the factory at recognised starting times of one minute (increased in certain special cases), after which the card racks are closed. This allowance does not apply to employees who enter subsequently, as they are late and subject to disciplinary penalties.

56. LEAVING WORKS DURING WORKING HOURS.

Employees may not leave the works during work hours without handing to the gatekeeper at the exit a permit in writing signed by their overlooker or section head.

57. FAILURE TO CLOCK.

Employees who fail on reaching or leaving work to record their time by means of their time cards and recording clocks as required by this rule will be warned verbally on the first occasion, and in writing on the second occasion ; in case of a third or subsequent omission in any calendar year they will be subject to the deduction of half an hour from their time.

Omissions to clock in will be reckoned separately from omissions to clock out.

58. LATES.

Employees will be admitted within half an hour after the recognised starting times subject to the exceptions recorded hereunder, but on each occasion the fact will be recorded and the employee debited with a " late," either " full " or " half."

Eight " full " lates or sixteen " half " lates are allowed to all employees in any one calendar year, and, in addition, eight " half " lates are allowed after either breakfast or tea in the same year, according to the following regulations.

The starting time lates are quite separate from the lates after breakfast and tea, and an employee using up the former lates may not draw on the latter, or *vice versa*.

In cases of lateness, cards should be stamped and placed in the box provided at the " in " board for that purpose.

Employees arriving late will be paid from the nearest quarter of an hour before they have clocked and will be expected to clock in as close as possible to their arranged starting time.

Provided that—

(*a*) In general, " half " lates are debited to workers due to commence work between midnight and 7.30 a.m., and " full " lates to those due to start between 7.30 a.m. and midnight, whether on shifts or day.

(*b*) Shift workers due in at 6.0 a.m. may clock in at any time up to 6.30 a.m., and those due in at 6.30 a.m. may clock in at any time up to 7 a.m. in either case by using half a " late," or at 7.30 a.m. by losing time without thereby using up one of their " lates."

(*c*) Employees (other than shift workers) who are asked to start at 7 a.m. or earlier may come in within half an hour by using up half a " late," or at 7.30 a.m. by losing time without thereby using up one of their " lates."

(*d*) Employees with continuous long service (*i.e.* ten years in the case of men, and seven years in the case of women) are not limited to eight " lates " in the year, but are allowed to come in up to thirty minutes after their recognised starting time on signing the special book kept in their department. This privilege may be withdrawn in individual cases if it is abused.

(*e*) Employees who by reason of having started

before 7.30 a.m. have taken a breakfast interval and have clocked in late within half an hour after the expiration of that interval; also those who are working beyond the normal finishing time of the factory and have clocked in late within half an hour after the expiration of the tea interval, will, in each instance, be debited with only half a " late."

(*f*) Employees travelling from Selby by train are allowed on eight occasions when they have missed the special train to the works to clock in within reasonable time after the arrival at York station of the next following train from Selby without a late being recorded.

(*g*) Employees (other than shift workers) working overtime later than 11.0 p.m. may clock in not later than 9.0 a.m. the following morning without any " late " being recorded, but they will not be paid for the time lost.

(*h*) An employee who, having put in his or her standard week by Friday night, is asked to come in on Saturday morning for the company's convenience will be admitted not later than half an hour after the recognised starting time without a " late " being recorded.

Note 1. Where, however, the Saturday morning forms part of the employee's standard week, the usual rules will apply.

Note 2. The one minute time allowance given after recognised starting time does not apply to " lates."

59. ADMISSION.

(*a*) In general, employees failing to arrive in the morning within the time allowed under Rule 58 will not be admitted until after dinner-time, and those failing to arrive after dinner time within the time allowed will not be admitted until the following morning.

(*b*) Morning shift workers will not be admitted after 7.30 a.m.

(*c*) Employees on afternoon or night shifts or permanent night work, who fail to clock in at the arranged time or within half an hour thereafter, will not be allowed in until half-way through their standard working period.

(d) Employees, other than shift workers, who are asked to start at 7 a.m. or earlier, will be admitted within the first half-hour ; in case of failing to do so they may, however, be admitted at 7.30 a.m., but not later.

(e) Workers who lose time by coming later than their arranged starting time will not receive overtime payment until the hours normal for that day have been worked. They will not be allowed to remain at work for the purpose of making up lost time unless the requirements of the section make this necessary.

60. ENTRANCES AND EXITS.

The entrances and exits available during ordinary factory hours are :—

    (a) South Time Office entrance.
    (b) Central Time Office   ,,
    (c) Fire Station   ,,
    (d) Card Box   ,,
    (e) Wigginton Road   ,,
    (f) South End of Main Corridor.

Outside ordinary factory hours the central time office entrance only is available. Special arrangements will be made when required for shift workers desiring to use the Wigginton Road entrance at 10 p.m. and 6 a.m., and for departments working overtime to use exits which are usually open only during ordinary factory hours.

SECTION H

SOCIAL

61. SALES OF GOODS TO EMPLOYEES.

Employees are allowed to purchase the company's manufactures up to a given amount each week on the clear understanding that such goods are not to be re-sold. Goods so purchased will be delivered to the purchasers on leaving and must not be taken back again into the factory.

62. Contact with Infectious Disease.

Where infectious disease occurs in an employee's home or lodgings, such employee must report particulars to the employment department at once, and must not enter the factory until written permission to return is given by the works doctor and shown to the employment department and time office. Such employees who are otherwise fit to return to work will receive wages at day rate in the case of day workers, and average piece rate in the case of piece-workers until the expiration of a period not exceeding five days from the day on which such report is made, or, in special cases, for such longer period as the works doctor certifies the absence to be necessary.

63. Application to Doctor, Dentist, Oculist, and Optician.

(*a*) Any factory employee wishing to consult the works doctor, dentist, oculist, or optician should inform his or her overlooker, who will put in the necessary requisition. Clerical workers should make application to the staff office.

(*b*) Employees returning to work after illness and desiring transfer to light work will be required to obtain the sanction of the works doctor.

(*c*) Seasonal, temporary, and casual workers may not receive treatment from either the dentist or optician, except with the consent of the appropriate employment officer.

64. Accidents.

Employees must immediately report to their overlooker any personal accident, even though the injury is only slight, such as a cut or bruise.

SECTION I

EDUCATION

65. School Classes.

Unless absent from work or excused by the works doctor, boys and girls are required to attend School

Continuation Classes in accordance with regulations made from time to time by the company after submission to and approval by the central works council.

66. No deductions from wages will be made on account of attendance at classes in the case of day workers, but bonus workers will receive no payment for the time they are at class.

SECTION J

CANTEEN

67. GIRLS' DINING-ROOM.

Girls desiring to do so may take their dinners into the gardens, but none of the company's crockery must be taken anywhere in the grounds except into the orchard, from which it must be returned to the girls' dining-room before work is resumed.

68. FREE TEA.

On nights when special overtime after six o'clock is being worked, tea (but not food) is provided in the dining-rooms for female employees, free of cost.

SECTION K

EMPLOYEE REPRESENTATION

69. THEFT.

All cases of alleged theft of property belonging to the company, or committed on or about the company's premises at York, will, after preliminary investigation, be referred to the theft committee set up for the purpose by the central works council. Any question as to whether a charge comes within this rule will be determined by the theft committee.

70. RIGHT OF APPEAL.

(a) Any person feeling that injustice has been done to him in connection with disciplinary action taken against

P

him under circumstances which do not give him the right to go to the appeal committee, has the right to appeal from the executive officer with regard to whose action he complains, to the executive officer immediately above him, and so on, if necessary right up to the chairman of the York Board, whose decision shall be final. The chairman will give his decision after consultation with the director of the function concerned, the labour director, and the trade union representative or employee making the appeal.

(*b*) An employee subjected to suspension, dismissal, or other disciplinary action—

(1) for breach of these Rules ;

(2) for conduct not affecting the performance of the work for which he or she is employed by the company; or

(3) by the theft committee

has a right of appeal to the appeal committee, which has power to determine whether the cause of complaint has occurred, and either to confirm, reduce, or increase the penalty.

(*c*) The management also has a right of appeal to the appeal committee against a decision of the theft committee on a charge made before it.

(*d*) Appeals from the theft committee to the appeal committee must be made within a reasonable time after the theft committee's decision.

(*e*) If, after a case has been dealt with by the appeal committee, fresh material evidence becomes available, either the individual concerned or the management may apply (to the theft committee if the case is one falling under para. (*b*) (3) or para. (*c*) of this Rule, or to the appeal committee in any other instance) for a re-hearing by the appeal committee, which may be granted if it is in the interests of justice that there should be a re-hearing. On such re-hearing the appeal committee will consist, as far as practicable, of the members who previously heard the case.

71. Appeal Committee.

The appeal committee consists of five persons, two appointed by the company and two appointed by the worker members of the central works council from amongst the employees of the company, with a chairman appointed by the other four members of the appeal committee. A reserve is appointed for each member of the appeal committee by the body appointing such member, and acts when the member is unable to do so. The appeal committee goes out of office on 31st March in each year, but the retiring committee has power to deal with any appeal which is pending when it goes out of office.

In addition to its powers under these Rules, the appeal committee determines any question referred to it by agreement between a director on behalf of the company and the employee or class of employees directly interested in such question. Questions not covered by this or the last preceding Rule will be dealt with by or under the direction of the board of directors as heretofore.

72. These Rules have been made by the company after submission to and approval by the central works council, and will remain in force until rescinded by the company. No alteration, except such as shall arise out of a revision or abrogation of the Industrial Agreement, shall be made therein without the express approval of the central works council, given at a meeting held after notice specifying that an alteration in the Rules will be considered thereat. Provided that any alteration or any new Rule made by the company and approved by the executive committee of the central council shall have effect temporarily until it can be submitted for the approval of the central council.

73. These Rules, with the exception of the following :—

1–5, 8, 23, 24(a), 26–31, 33–43, 45(a), 48–50, 52, 53(c), 56, 60–64, 67–74,

do not apply to clerks.

74. Subject to Rule 73 and to any other exceptions contained in the Rules, all the Rules apply to the whole of the company's employees working on or about the

P*

company's premises at York, unless·specifically excluded by the terms of their engagement. They are only intended to regulate the conduct of employees generally towards each other and the company in matters arising or capable of arising constantly in the course of the company's business.

ROWNTREE & CO., LTD.

C. FANTHORPE, Secretary.

Approved by the Central Works Council,

A. SIMPSON, Chairman.

G. S. CROSSLEY, Vice-Chairman.

APPENDIX VI

SECTION I

THE firm of Rowntree & Co. Ltd., into whose service you have just entered, has a world-wide reputation which has been built up on two solid foundations :—

(*a*) The quality and reasonable price of the goods manufactured.

(*b*) The care taken by the company to safeguard the interests of its employees.

The company desires that your life here in the factory shall be spent under the happiest and best possible conditions, and that the goods which you are helping to produce shall be pure and wholesome.

We ask you to help us to make this possible by giving the company your willing co-operation and by doing your work at all times to the best of your ability. Happy and smooth working conditions can only be secured if you follow rules and instructions and join your overlookers and fellow-workers in pulling together for the good of your section and of the company as a whole. Success in these directions depends upon your knowledge of what is required and upon your willingness to help. The latter depends upon yourself ; to help you to understand what we want we have prepared this leaflet of information, rules, and instructions.

QUALITY.

The quality for which the name of Rowntree is known is only secured when every sweet is thoroughly wholesome and of the right flavour, size, shape, and colour.

One of the chief ways in which you can help to maintain the good name of Rowntree is always to be on the look-out to prevent anything other than the proper ingredients becoming mixed with our goods. Unless the greatest care is taken, it is possible for bits of wood, metal, hair, pins, nails, screws, or other foreign substances to fall into goods. The presence of such things in our sweets is likely to be dangerous to customers who eat them and would seriously injure our reputation and trade —thus throwing employees out of work. You are, there-fore, asked always to be particularly careful to see that there is no chance for anything to get into the sweets or materials which you are handling.

Articles not allowed in the Workrooms.

It is strictly forbidden to take into the workrooms—

(a) Pins, needles, powder, any article made of glass or other brittle substance, or anything else which the management considers might get into the goods. (In an emergency, a needle and cotton may be borrowed on application to your overlooker.)

(b) Dinner baskets, bags, or similar receptacles. These and other small articles (bicycle lamps, bags containing lunch, etc.) must be put in the place appointed by your department.

(c) Chewing-gum, and strong smelling food—such as oranges.

Scented hair-oil should not be used, as chocolate may be tainted in this way.

Moth and Grub.

Unless the utmost care is taken, a considerable amount of damage may be done to our goods by moths which breed in the cocoa beans. The only certain way of getting rid of this trouble is to destroy all moths, and you are asked to kill every moth you see, and to report to your over-looker whenever you see any sign of them.

Waste.

We can only maintain or increase our trade if we manu-facture at a reasonable price. It is important, therefore, that no one should waste time or materials in the workrooms. All sweets should be handled with care. Workers are asked to avoid dropping them on the floor, for sweets on the floor mean untidiness and loss of money.

The taking of chocolate, sweets, or ingredients, the property of the company, whether with a view to eating them on the premises or otherwise disposing of them, is strictly forbidden and is in most cases punished by dismissal. It may seem a small matter for a worker to take an occasional sweet, but it would cost the company over £800 a year if each worker took only one sweet a day.

Loss of time when at work is another form of waste. Employees must start work promptly when the bell rings, but not before, and they must not cease work until the time officially fixed for their department.

Betting, taking part in raffles or sweepstakes, and the playing of any game of chance for money on any part of the company's premises are prohibited.

SAFETY FIRST.

It is essential if accidents are to be avoided that you should always obey instructions regarding the use of machinery. The cleaning of machinery when in motion is strictly forbidden, and there are safety devices to prevent injury to workers on machines. But the most important thing is that you yourself should be careful. Forgetfulness, carelessness, or disobedience to instructions may result in serious accidents despite all possible precautions on the part of the company.

Always be alert to these dangers. Never interfere with machinery that does not concern you. If you do not thoroughly understand your own machine, ask your overlooker about it. Do not ride on bogies in the corridors. Never push your fellow-workers roughly about ; care is particularly necessary when leaving work, when going downstairs or passing machinery. Cultivate the " Safety First " habit.

HEALTH.

Unnecessary absence from work should be avoided. It prevents smooth running in the factory and is a serious loss to the workers as well as to the company.

Seasonal and casual workers have to pass a modified medical examination, but must pass the full medical test before being taken on to the regular staff. Employees are able to obtain attention daily from the doctor. Every personal accident, however slight, such as a cut or a bruise, must be reported at once to the overlooker, in order to avoid any trouble which may result from the neglect of a small injury. Under certain conditions, of which you may be informed by the employment department, employees may obtain attention from the dentist and the visiting optician.

Employees visiting the doctor, dentist, or optician, and any who, by reason of illness or other sufficient cause, are detained in a rest room, will receive payment for the time so spent at minimum day rates in the case of piece-workers and at ordinary rates in the case of day workers.

Employees sent home by the doctor, or going home with the doctor's permission after an accident at the works, receive payment at the rate of their average earnings for the time lost on the day on which they are sent home.

In order to avoid the spread of infection, an employee in whose home or lodging an infectious disease occurs must report particulars to the employment department at once, and must *not* enter the workroom on any condition until written permission to return to work has been given by the works doctor and shown to the employment department and time office. Such employees who are otherwise fit to return to work receive wages at day rate in the case of day workers, and average piece rate in the case of piece-workers, for a period of not more than five days from the day on which the infectious disease was reported, or in special circumstances for a longer period if the works doctor certifies such absence to be necessary.

Except in cases of illness or other serious emergency, you may not stay away from work without having previously obtained an official permit. These permits must be left at the time office or with the gatekeeper. If you are unable to come to work, you should at once send a written explanation to the manager or, in the case of clerks, to the staff office.

Unless absent from work or excused by the works doctor, boys and girls are required to attend Day Continuation Classes in accordance with regulations made from time to time by the company after submission to and approval by the central works council.

SECTION II

WAGES AND HOLIDAYS.

(*a*) *Annual Holiday*. In addition to the statutory holidays provided for in the Factory Acts, an annual holiday with pay is given to employees. The length of holiday will be in proportion to service as follows (the period of service being counted from 31st July, or, in the case of the building department, 30th April, in each year) :—

	Holiday Allowance.
Less than six months' continuous service	None.
Six months' and under seven months' continuous service	$2\frac{1}{2}$ days.
With half a day for each additional month up to :—	
Eleven months' continuous service	One week.

(*b*) *Bank Holidays*. Payment will be made each year for four Bank Holidays and for Christmas Day and Good Friday, and will be allowed to all employees on the company's books on the holiday in question, and also to employees who leave on the last preceding working day before such holiday or within forty-eight hours before such last working day and have been in the company's service for at least six months immediately preceding their leaving.

In respect of holidays, piece and bonus workers receive I.I.R.C. minimum day rates, and day workers their ordinary day rates.

LEAVE FOR YORK RACES.

In departments where conditions of work will allow, leave of absence is granted both to male and female employees, for one afternoon selected by the management, but no leave of absence can be granted for any of the other days. Application must be made not less than three clear days before the afternoon selected.

SECTION III

DISCIPLINE.

Lates.

Employees will be admitted within half an hour after the recognised starting time subject to certain exceptions, but on each occasion the fact will be recorded and the employee debited with a late, either " full " or " half." Eight " full " lates or sixteen " half " lates are allowed to employees within any one calendar year. You should read carefully Rule 58, which gives full particulars of these arrangements. (The Works Rules can be obtained in full from all overlookers.)

Cleanliness.

All employees must wash their hands thoroughly before handling foodstuffs, especially before returning to work after visiting the lavatory. Spitting on the company's premises is forbidden. Snuff-taking and the chewing of tobacco and chewing-gum in workrooms are forbidden.

Bicycles.

Bicycles must not at any time be ridden up or down the Time Office Avenues or the road on the north side of the gum department fruit rooms.

Sales inside the Factory.

The sale, in the works or offices, of watches, jewellery, photographs, Christmas cards, etc., is not allowed.

Emergency Exit Doors.

Emergency exit doors must not be used except in cases of fire or other emergency.

Change of Address.

Employees changing their addresses must notify at once their overlooker.

Theft.

All cases of alleged theft of property belonging to the company, or committed on or about the company's premises at York, will after preliminary investigation be referred to the theft committee set up for the purpose by the central works council. Any question as to whether a charge comes within this Rule is determined by the theft committee.

Right of Appeal.

An employee subjected to suspension, dismissal, or other disciplinary action—

(*a*) for breach of the Works Rules ;
(*b*) for conduct not affecting the performance of the work for which he or she is employed by the company ; or
(*c*) by the theft committee

has a right of appeal to the appeal committee, which has power to determine whether the cause of complaint has occurred and either to confirm, reduce, or increase the penalty.

SECTION IV

Social.

Works Councils.

A central works council and departmental councils have been set up to enable representatives of the management to meet representatives of the workers for the discussion of many matters. All employees who are over eighteen years of age and have been in the company's employ for six months are eligible to vote for representatives on these councils.

Unemployment Benefit Scheme.

The firm's Unemployment Benefit Scheme applies to all persons, male and female, between the ages of eighteen and pension age who, immediately prior to their unemployment, have been in the employ of the company for a continuous period of six months.

To be eligible for benefit an applicant must, immediately prior to his unemployment, have contributed for a minimum period of six months to a trade union or other society approved by the company, a sum of not less than 2d. per week for the purpose of assuring a weekly or other periodical payment supplementary to the firm's unemployment benefit.

Further particulars may be obtained from the Staff Office or the Men's Employment Department.

Trade Unions.

While recognising that it is entirely a matter for the employee's own judgment as to whether he shall or shall not join a trade union, the opinion of the directors is " that it is desirable in the interests of the company and its employees that the latter shall be suitably organised and that membership of a trade union is, in the general case, desirable."

Education.

The company encourages employees to improve their education. Anyone who desires help or advice about a particular course of study should apply to the Education Officer, Employment Block.

Suggestion Scheme.

Suggestions for any improvements in the works are cordially invited and prizes are given monthly for good suggestions. Suggestion boxes and forms are placed in the corridors.

Keep Fit Classes, Clubs, etc.

If you would like to join any of these classes or clubs, you should ask your overlooker, or write to Miss Sherlock, Women's Social Department ; Mr. H. W. Locke, Education Department ; or Mr. B. P. Rowntree, Men's Employment Department.

J.R. Library.

This library was set up to honour the memory of the founder of the business, Joseph Rowntree. It is free, and you are invited to make use of it.

Hospital Contributory Scheme.

You may join the Hospital Contributory Scheme, whereby by paying 2d. or 3d. a week regularly you and certain of your dependants may receive free hospital treatment. These contributions may, with your consent, be deducted from your wages. For fuller particulars and application forms you should apply to the Men's Employment Department.

Employees' Holiday Fund and Savings Bank.

You may save for your holidays by having as much as you wish deducted weekly from your wages and deposited in the Bank, to be drawn by you before the annual holiday. If you wish to join this fund, ask your overlooker for the necessary form.

If you wish to save by joining the weekly Savings Bank, look out for the collector when he or she comes round on Friday afternoons.

The Works Sick Club (for Women).

Girls may join the sick club, particulars of which can be obtained from the Secretary, Women's Employment Department.

The Buying of the Company's Goods.

Arrangements are made for employees to buy limited quantities of the company's goods for their own or family's use at a special cheap rate on the understanding that such goods are not to be re-sold. Order forms are supplied weekly by overlookers. Goods so purchased are delivered to the purchasers on leaving, and must not be taken back again into the factory.

If at any time you are in any difficulty do not hesitate to ask for help. You can get this from the employment departments, who will put you in touch with the person who can help you most usefully. If you are a trade unionist, your shop steward may be able to help.

ROWNTREE & CO. LTD.

INDEX

239